The story of
CROMER PIER

Poppyland Publishing

'Rages and surges' of the sea have 'swallowed uppe & drownded' a great many houses in Cromer. The 'inhabitants hathe to their grete and importunate charges defended [the town] by making a grete peers, and dayle putte to insatiable charges.'
The Bishop of Norwich (Thomas Thirlby) and others, 1551.

'What is 75 years old, cold, draughty, noisy, expensive to run and stuck out in the North Sea? 'Cromer pier, of course, and according to a report it looks as if it will always be a white elephant. . . .'
North Norfolk News, 27th February 1976, p.1.

'The Commissioners have embedded in their scheme all the best points of other piers, and carefully excluded everything that would lower the tone of the place.'
A. E. Jarvis, at the opening of the present pier in June 1901.

'Cromer's present pier is something of a crowning glory. . . . The pier has never made a penny profit, but preserving this relic is vital if Cromer is to remain a proper seaside resort. Piers are an endangered species and Cromer is like a natural habitat.'
Martin Warren, Cromer, p.10.

George Robey joked there. Semprini played there. John Heddle Nash sang there. Damaged by ships and contractors' rigs, wrecked by the sea times without number, Cromer pier has been repaired and rebuilt again and again, and survives with its now-flourishing end-of-the-pier show. Here is its story, in the words of those who have loved it and despaired of it during more than six centuries.

Compiled by Christopher Pipe
at Watermark,
Norfolk House, Hamilton Road, Cromer NR27 9HL
Copyright © 1998 Christopher Pipe
ISBN 0 946148 52 X

First published 1998
by Poppyland Publishing
13 Kings Arms Street, North Walsham NR28 9JX
Printed by Printing Services (Norwich) Ltd.

The publishers would be interested to hear from anyone who can supplement this history with old photographs, programmes or other documents.

ACKNOWLEDGEMENTS
Thanks are due to Nigel Stewart, pier theatre manager 1995-97, for first suggesting this book, and to the following for their help: the library staff of Eastern Counties Newspapers; David Beasley, Librarian at Goldsmiths' Hall in London; Norma J. Crowe of the Rochester upon Medway Studies Centre; the staff of Norfolk County Libraries and of the Norfolk County Record Office; Peter Stibbons of Poppyland Publishing, for his help with the illustrations; Martin Warren and Alistair Murphy of Cromer Museum; Rona Carswell, Bernard Polley and Max Tyler, for copies of old programmes; David Ventress of Dossor East; and Beryl Woodhouse for her newspaper cuttings, programmes and personal memories as well as her notes from the minutes of the Cromer Protection Commissioners who employed both her father and her grandfather on the pier.

Cover photo: Dr Chris Croton

The extract from *The Kingdom by the Sea* is copyright © Paul Theroux 1983, and is reproduced with permission of Penguin Books Ltd.

Every effort has been made to trace copyright owners, but the publishers would be pleased to hear from any party whose rights may inadvertently have been infringed.

CONSTRUCTION AND PURPOSE

CONTENTS

CONSTRUCTION AND PURPOSE

Outline chronology

The chronology is necessarily incomplete, especially for the earlier years.

c.1391	First pier built
1580s	Pier rebuilt, of timber
1607	The pier has disappeared again. Officials reject the idea of a single large structure, preferring several smaller piers
1664	Cromer issues a national appeal for help in repairing both pier and church
c.1732	Pier company begins to rebuild the pier
1820	Pier washed away in a storm
1821-2	New jetty constructed, using cast iron supports
1836	Jetty damaged in storm; small portion at the land end soon rebuilt with iron stanchions presenting a flat surface to the sea
1845	All except the recent landward section washed away by a storm
1846	New pier built of timber, with sloping piles
1854	End damaged by brig *Marsingale*; temporary repairs
1860	Restored to full length
1890	Last three supports damaged (they were replaced by cast iron ones)
1897	Wrecked by storm and dismantled
1901	Present pier opened
1905	Bandstand area covered to form pavilion
1923	Lifeboat house opened at end of pier
1940	Centre section of pier destroyed as part of war defences
1950	Pavilion Theatre reopened. Temporary pay box at pier entrance
1951	Shops & pay box rebuilt
1976	Listed as a building of historical and architectural interest
1990	Amusement arcade blown away by storm, and not replaced
1993	Tayjack rig demolishes part of the pier
1996	Lifeboat house demolished to make way for larger replacement

6

The earliest piers

The earliest mention of Cromer Pier - in Letters Patent of 1390. The word 'Crowmere' is the fifth word in the third line, and 'pere' is the tenth word in the second line. This is the earliest known document which uses the word 'pier' in its modern sense.

What the earliest piers were used for

Salt fish

The north Norfolk ports were 'noted for cod, ling and orgeys. . . . The provision of salt fish had become a well-established industry by the beginning of the fourteenth century.' Salt fish was needed to feed the growing populations of cities (especially London), and to supply the king's 'armies whilst campaigning overseas. Cromer was one of the Norfolk towns to supply salt fish to the Black Prince for provisioning his army in the middle of the fourteenth century. So important was salt fish to the nation's diet that Norfolk fishing boats were exempt from naval service (in an age which had no permanent navy).

Pirates

'The practice of fishing in convoys is well documented. In 1436 a licence was given to the fishermen of the towns of Blakeney and Cromer "to put to sea with 24 of their vessels appointed for fishing this season, any arrest on such vessels not withstanding, provided always that their master keep their vessels continually in company." Whatever the economic advantages of fishing in convoy, it was primarily adopted for security from attack from pirates or nations at war with England.'

In 1404, after a lot of trouble from pirates and privateers of the Hanse towns, 'the mariners of Cley and Cromer were granted a licence "to go to sea with 10 vessels and boats furnished with fencible men, artillers and victuals at their own costs to resist the King's enemies for the safety of the coasts and ports there."' Later the same year, a dogger from Cromer was among nine vessels, with hired soldiers aboard, which attacked two foreign vessels and seized their cargo; but they had to repay the merchants and add 60% damages. The next month, however, it was reported that Cromer sailors were among those who seized two Dutch ships and brought them back, one to Scarborough and the other to Blakeney, to sell, having thrown 36 merchants and mariners into the sea.

About 1407, there were Cromer men among 100 fishermen who were captured, bound and thrown into the sea by Hanseatic merchants in Norway.

Iceland

'The trade [with Iceland] seems to have started, quite suddenly, early in the fifteenth century and legend has it that Robert Bacon, a Cromer fisherman, "discovered" Iceland at this time. . . . It is complete nonsense to assume that Bacon stumbled upon an unknown isle . . . [but] in 1262 Iceland was united with Norway and it was not long before all trade to Iceland was ordered to go from Bergen where the Norwegian kings exacted exorbitant taxes. . . . British trade with Iceland died out and by the end of the fourteenth century there are no records of any British ships visiting Iceland. The Icelandic fishery had certainly been popular earlier in the fourteenth century.

'By the turn of the fifteenth century, political conditions were changing. Iceland, since the Union of Kalmar in 1397, was now under the domination of Denmark, and seemingly being ignored by Danes and Norwegians alike as the Annals complained of a lack of ships. Also at this time English fishermen were going to Norway to fish her waters and import her fish. In 1383 an ancient petition mentions that "fishers of salt fish of Cromer and Blakeney" were fishing off the coasts of Norway and Denmark. However, by the beginning of the fifteenth century the Hanseatic League had gained much influence in Bergen, and they did all in their power, by means of taxes, laws and force, to prevent the English from having anything to do with the Norwegian fish trade. The result was that the English ignored the Bergen monopoly and started to trade directly with Iceland and were welcomed by the Icelanders who had been neglected by their fellow Scandinavians. Thus it was quite possible that Robert Bacon, who was obviously an enterprising man, may have been the first, or one of the first, to head once again for Icelandic waters. . . .

'It was between the years 1412-1420 that the "rediscovered" Icelandic trade began to bloom again and it remained strong for the next two centuries, especially with the east coast ports who continued going to Iceland long after the men of Bristol and the west country were turning their attentions to the newly discovered fisheries off the Newfoundland coast. . . . An inquiry in 1528 listed Blakeney, Cley and Cromer as having 30 Iceland ships, the same number as Yarmouth.'

Hooton, The Glaven Ports , pp.30, 32, 37, 52-55, 64-66, 71.

1390

'Shortly before 1391, the inroads of the sea, which had fifty years before swallowed up the church and churchyard, rendered the navigation so dangerous that a pier was commenced for the safety and defence of ships and (fishing) boats in the market or port called Crowmere, as we are told in the preamble to certain Letters Patent, dated at Westminster, 2nd Dec. 14 Ric. II., whereby the king granted to the men of Shipden the right of levying for five years certain duties on all merchandise coming to their port, in aid of making such pier. . . . The list of articles is a curious one, the chief imports apparently being herrings, salt, rygolds . . . , wainscot, and tunholt (all by the hundred), pitch and turpentine (in barrel), oil (in barrel), fir spars (by the hundred), dascells (by the thousand), ferri (nails? by the thousand), corn and malt, sea coal (by the chaldron), fish called "orgoys", lob, ling, and cod. Everything worth five shillings was liable to this duty, except wool, leather, skins covered with wool, lead, tin, and wine.'

Rye, Cromer Past and Present, pp.47-48. "Rygolds", or rigalds, were spars of wood; tunholt was wood for making barrels. "Orgoys", or orgays, were organ ling, a large kind of ling; "lob" was pollack. The salt would have been needed for salting the fish.

1453-1535

'This pier was long a sore expense to the men of Shipden and Cromer, and for a series of years it would be hard to find a will made by an inhabitant of either place that does not contain a bequest to it.'

Rye, 'Notes on the Port and Trade of Cromer,' p.278.

A reconstruction by Cromer photographer and artist Philip Vicary, based on his observation of foundations exposed when the beach was scoured away. The Elizabethan pier could well have looked something like this, although the extant timbers are more likely to be part of the 1731 pier. An alternative interpretation suggests that the angled section was the remains of a groyne, not part of the pier. Compare picture on p.16 and plan on p.47. (P. A. Vicary)

'From various wills of the inhabitants, it is clear that the old pier - by which we must understand a jetty, or "work," enclosing an actual, if small, harbour in which ships could ride, which had been begun about 1391, had been continued partly by the duties the inhabitants had been authorized to levy on merchandise, partly by a rate (see will of John Mason, 1487) and partly by legacies. The keeper of the pier is mentioned in the will of Robert Hayles, vicar, 1479.'

At least a couple of dozen wills in this period include bequests for the repair of the pier. One person, John Sparks, in 1483 left a legacy to place 'great stones' - i.e., to support the pier as a breakwater.

Rye, Cromer Past and Present, pp.51, 56-57.

1551

The Privy Council were petitioned on 12th January by the Bishop of Norwich and others, who said that the 'rages and surges' of the sea had recently 'swallowed uppe & drownded' a great many houses. The 'inhabitants hathe to their grete and importunate charges defended [the town] by making a grete peers, and dayle putte to insatiable charges.'

Quoted by Walter Rye in 'Cromer Pier,' Eastern Counties Collectanea I (1873), pp.37-39. Here the pier seems to be a defensive measure against coastal erosion.

1579

'January 31. "To all justyces of peace, mayors, sheriefs, bayliefs, constables, customers, comtrollers and serchers, and all other offycers, mynisters and subjectes of our sovereigne ladye the Quenes Majesty", we the pier-reeves and inhabitants of Cromer alias Shipden send greetings. The Queen by her letters patent of 2 January 1578/9 has granted us through our appointed deputies, factors and assignees to buy and provide within the county of Norfolk 8,000 quarters of malt, barley, beans and peas and 2,000 quarters of wheat, and "after suche Her Majestes customes and other duties for the same payed and fullye aunswered as was accustomablye payed in the tenthe yere of her highnes reigne" to export the same from the ports of Lynn and Yarmouth or their member creeks in any ship and to any places overseas in amity with Her Majesty. "Know ye now therefore that we the said peer-riefs and inhabitants of Cromer" do authorise Rychard Peereson, merchant, and his assignees or deputies to buy and ship 100 quarters of wheat within five years after the date of the letters patent "or within twoe yeres then next ymmediyatelye ensuynge after the said fyve yeres".'

Bacon, Papers, vol.II, 1578-1585, p.30.

1580

The will of Dyones Flegge, dated 8th August, gave 40 shillings for 'the buildinge maynteyninge and repayringe of the late begonne and erected Piere'.

Rye, 'Cromer Pier,' Eastern Counties Collectanea I (1873), pp. 38-39.

1582

'On 4 July, 1582, Queen Elizabeth granted letters patent to the inhabitants of Cromer to transport (export) 20,000 quarters of wheat, barley, and malt for the maintenance of their town, and towards the building of an "ould decayed peere" there. Thomas Baxter, gent., was appointed to sell the license for the benefit of the town, and pay the proceeds to the "Pier-reeves" - such as the inhabitants should yearly choose according to an ancient custom among them to be bestowed upon the pier, they accounting monthly to Baxter and the other inhabitants, and Baxter in turn delivering such accounts to the Barons of the Exchequer, "so that the 'balance' (illusory idea) should remain to her majesty."'

Rye, Cromer Past and Present, pp.59-60. A similar arrangement had recently been made to finance the rebuilding of Dover pier.

In 1936 R. W. Ketton-Cremer found the seal of Cromer Pier at Felbrigg Hall. Ashe Windham of Felbrigg Hall was one of the subscribers to the 1731 pier, but the spelling 'pere' suggests a date for the seal not later than the sixteenth century. Ketton-Cremer presented the seal to the Council on the occasion of the reopening of the pier in 1951, and it is now in Cromer Museum.

(Drawing: Martin Warren)

1589

There are accounts of wages paid and materials purchased for the rebuilding of Cromer pier. The pier-reeves were Robert Cotterell, gentleman, and John Daynes, mariner.

Bacon, Papers, vol. III, 1586-1595 , pp.77-79, 82.

1591

A petition from Robert Clarke to the Chancellor of the Exchequer and others complains that various sums of money paid to the pier reeves 'doe remayne in the hands of Emanuell Callyarde' and various others 'which have byn peerereves and who doth refuse to make payment therof', and that Robert Underwood 'did by Indirect meanes gett into his possession to the value of fower hundred pounds wch he did never make payment of or bestowe uppon the sayd peere being for that purpose gyven'.

Rye, Cromer Past and Present, pp.lvi-lxi, quotes the full text of the documents concerned.

A harbour at Sheringham

'At Sheringham, a small harbour was constructed with north, east and west piers to make the haven safer for the fishermen. Not only did they have much trouble in building the harbour, and several disputes with the contractors, but the fishermen complained that it caused currents which silted up the channels by which they brought their boats up to the beach. Also the sea resented its presence, causing numerous repairs to be made, so that in the end the harbour was demolished and short jetties erected instead.'

Hooton, The Glaven Ports , p.76.

In March 1593 the inhabitants of Sheringham and Beeston wrote to Secretary Wolley. They were chief traders for the Iceland fishing of ling and cod. They said the pier building on that part of the coast was preventing the further washing away of houses there by the rage of the sea, and if finished, would be a great safeguard for ships.

Calendar of State Papers Domestic, Eliz. ccxliv.112.

1590s

'A note of all shuch somes of money as I George England have receauved and hade of John Blowfild for and towardes the preparacon of the peare of Cromer and layd out as is here after mencioned as followethe

                                                                    20 *li*

The document clearly says 'preparacon', but probably means 'reparation' or repair.

'Imp'mis to Robert Smith and Nicholasse
Bacon for worke donne about the peare   vj *li* xiiij *s*

'It[em] delivered to John Sadler to the use of the peare   40 *s*

'It more to John Springold beinge another of
the peare reauves   40 *s*

'It to Robert Dobbe [*or* Hobbe], Robert Smithe and Thomas
Amis for worke donne about the peare   x *s* viij *d*

'It to Mr Roger Windham for the growndedge [*i.e.*, bottom?] of
a shippe wh[ich] was Bought for plankes for yᵉ peare   xiiij *s*

'It to Robert Springold that he laid out
for plankes for the peare   xvij *s* x *d*

'It to the same Robert for his boate to feche
them home   ij *s* ij *d*

Robert Springold's will was proved in 1597-98.

'It to John shortinge for fillinge fower
huches in the peare   xiij *s* iiij *d*

The hutches were probably wooden cribs which had to be filled with stones.

'It to gardiner beinge one of the peare Reaues
to the use of the peare   50 *s*

'It to Willm Rye for worke that he tooke in hand to doo   x *s*

William Rye's will was proved in 1603.

'It laid out for xvj pound of hempe
to make a roppe for the fframe   ij *s* viij *d*

Government action in the reign of Queen Elizabeth provided temporary encouragement for the growing of hemp, which was appreciated locally as providing useful jobs for the poor; and even as late as 1851 Cromer had its own ropemaker.

'It to Mr Alling as for knowledge of a
satisfaccon for the execution of Blowfild   vj *s*

'It for two sparres[?] for the Peare   iiij *s* iiij *d*

'It to Nicholasse Willson for xvij dayes worke
at the peare after xvj *d* the daye   xxij *s* viij *d*

'It to him for his manne for xviij dayes
after xiiij *d* the daye   xxi *s*

'It to him for one tide   viij *d*

'Tide' here means the amount of time during which the height of the water allowed work to be done.

'It to him for ij mene viij dayes   xviij *s* viij *d*

'It for eyther of thē [*i.e.*, for each of them] a tide   xvi *d*

'It to Bacon for eight dayes worke
about the peare   ix *s* viij *d*

                    Sùm totalitʳ   20 *lib* 19 *s'*

Account of monies received from John Blowfield and paid out by George England for work done on the pier. George England (who had become a pier reeve by 1591) has received £20 from John Blowfield, and this is his account of how he has spent it. (He has received £20 and paid out £20.19s. - the arithmetic, despite its disconcerting mixture of roman and arabic numbers, works out exactly.) The account is undated, but several of the names appear in other documents of the 1590s, and George England seems to have died about 1602.

1607

The inhabitants of Cromer having petitioned for help, Sir Nathaniel Bacon, JP, visited the town together with James Calthorp and John Kemp. They examined witnesses and saw for themselves the cliffs and the evidence of erosion.

The advantages of having a pier at Cromer were listed as:
1. It protected the town from erosion by the sea.
2. It was a place of safety for mariners in distress. This included Cromer men in their small boats, and also fishermen from other parts, and even from abroad, who came here for the herrings. Since the decay of the old pier, 'manye hunderds' of fishermen and passengers 'have perished besydes the loss of their goods'.
3. It was likewise a safe refuge for ships being pursued by enemy craft during wartime.
4. It made it far cheaper to get goods to the surrounding countryside, the nearest port now being more than ten miles away.

Bacon and his colleagues found that the sea 'hath brought to ruine manie howses ther, and hath utterly decaied a peere, wch was built not long since of tymber wth great chardge. . . . The helpe must be eyther in making a great peere, wch maie be the safety both of the towne and small ships, or in making severall smalle peers of jetties wch can only succour ye towne.' In their report, dated 22nd October 1607, they recommended the latter, since they were frightened of the cost of erecting and maintaining a large structure. They were also influenced by the fact that much of the money from the 1582 licence had remained unused, or was 'converted to private uses'.

Bacon, Official Papers (Camden 3rd series, 26), pp.124-126.

1664

'The first register [of this village church in Derbyshire] contains many records of Tissington's response to the many "briefs" of that period. "Briefs" were appeals made by various towns or churches for financial help in a crisis of some sort.' One entry reads:

'4th December, 1664 - collected then towards the repair of the Pier and the Parish Church of Cromer in the county of Norfolk, the sum of four shillings and fourpence.'

A Short History of Tissington and its Parish Church, p.15. Other parishes which are known to have responded to this brief include Badsey (Warwickshire), 3s, Old Newton (Suffolk), 5s. 6d, The pier seems not to have lasted much longer, for it is not shown at all on a map of 1717.

1676

'On 30th October 1676 Blakeney and Cley were visited by several officers of the crown who were there to set out the official limits of the port and to establish where the official quays were, and where goods were to be loaded and unloaded, in an attempt to regulate trade and make the excise officers' jobs a little easier. The official limits of the port ran from Morston Sluice in the west (the boundary with the port of Wells) as far as Cromer church in the east, which was the start of the limits of Yarmouth. More importantly they began to "assign and appoint the several open place and places . . . for the loading or shipping of any goods, wares or merchandizes" as the official language of the Special Commission put it. The favoured landing places chosen were "Mr. Burton's key or Wharfe" (67ft by 36ft) and "Simon Britif's Key or Wharfe" (138ft by 36ft) both in Cley. These were now the only legal places to carry on trade and consequently the commissioners "utterly prohibit, . . . and debarr all other places within the said port of Blakeney and Cley from the privilege, right and benefitt of a place, Key or Wharfe for the landing or discharging, ladeing or shipping of any Good, Wares or Merchandises." It was now illegal to use any other quay or bank for loading or unloading. . . .

'However, some time during the eighteenth century the coffin was prised open and trade was resurrected at Blakeney regardless of any Special Commission. . . . It probably occurred later in the century, simply as a result of the increase in coastal trade. The official quays at Cley could not cope and the excise men would have had to accept this. . . The Commissioners were back in 1738 redefining the limits of the port but not mentioning any official landing places.'

Hooton, The Glaven Ports , pp.160-161.

Yarmouth proposes a drastic solution

Cromer was not the only pier in need of expensive repair about this time. Yarmouth council, faced with a similar problem, came up with what seemed to them the ideal practical solution. This was in Cromwell's day, when bishops were out of fashion and it was the Mayor who sat in the bishop's chair. Yarmouth's proposal was simple, if drastic: demolish Norwich cathedral! In 1650 they petitioned Parliament to grant them 'such a part of the lead and other usefull materials of that vast and altogether useless Cathedral in Norwich, towards the building of a works house to employ our almost starved poor, and repairing our peeres!'

Ketton-Cremer, R. W. Forty Norfolk Essays. Norwich: Jarrold, 1961.

The eighteenth century

'The improvements in farming, often referred to as the Agricultural Revolution, many of which were pioneered in Norfolk, ensured that there was a growing surplus available for export. London, by far the largest city at the beginning of the century, continued to grow and its unceasing demand for food could no longer be supplied by the Home Counties alone, but spread out further into East Anglia. Road transport was still in its infancy and coastal shipping, despite the appalling number of ships regularly lost each year, was still the cheapest, quickest and most reliable way of transporting bulky goods.'

Hooton, The Glaven Ports , pp.166-167. Cromer's granary (which still survives at the top of the Gangway) was built some time after 1747 and converted into coastguard cottages between 1836 and 1843.

1731

'On 17 Jan. 1731, a deed . . . recites that proposals had been made, and an undertaking was then on foot for making and erecting a pier, or some other security, for the safe riding and lodging of ships or small vessels, as well for the importation, as also for the exportation of corn, coal, and other goods, wares, and merchandises, for the doing whereof several parcels of wood and timber and other materials must be had and purchased, and great sums of money laid out and expended, as well for these as for other purposes; and that after the same was completed, a toll or duty by way of tonnage must be laid upon and paid for all corn coals, and other goods, &c., for maintaining and keeping the said pier or place for the lodging and riding the said ships and vessels in good repair, order, and condition, for doing which an Act of Parliament must be had and obtained. Also that the management of the undertaking had been committed to Richard Ellis, of N. Repps (steward of the manor), Bozoon Briggs, of Bradfield, Richard Smith, of Cromer, and William Claydon, of Paston, gentleman.

'A covenant is inserted by the managers to expend all monies they shall receive on the work, and that all who subscribe not less than £10 towards the undertaking, should have free liberty of ingress and regress to and from the sea-shore of Cromer in over and upon the Gangles or road now belonging to them leading from the king's highway, leading from the new (new?) mansion house of him the said Richard Smith, down to the said shore for fifty years. Voting is to be one vote for £20, two for £40, three for £60, and so on.

'Those who executed the deed were -

H. Harbord	£100.	Wm. Claydon	£20.
A. Windham	£100.	Richd. Smith	£20.
F. Wyndham	£100.	R. Ellis & Compy.	£20.
Edm. Jewell	£20.	James Weld (?)	£20.
Richard Ellis	£20.	William Goate	£20.
Bozoon Brigge	£20.	John Kirby	£20.
Pat. St. Clair	£20.		

'The deed had seals for sixty-one subscribers, but the above thirteen - unlucky number! - were all that subscribed, and I expect the project came to nothing. I never heard of any Act being obtained, though probably the work was actually begun, for . . . in the disputes about the boundaries of the manor of Cromer Gunners, in 1764, one witness spoke of the pier having been begun about thirty-two years before, which would be 1732.'

'The promoters of the pier lost no time in trying to promote the trade, for in 1731-2, they got leave first to discharge coal and cinders, then to export corn, and lastly, to ship and land coast goods generally.'

Rye, Cromer Past and Present, pp.68-70. The Ellis family owned Northrepps Hall; Goat and Kirby owned sea-front properties in Cromer; the Harbords owned Gunton Hall; Patrick St Clair was the Rector of Metton and Felbrigg, and had been prevailed upon to sign in order to encourage other clergymen to subscribe; the Wyndhams owned Cromer Hall; the Windhams, of Felbrigg Hall, owned the land next to the Gangway.

1732

'The subscriptions of Cromer flag very much, and I do not hear any hath done it since I did.'

Patrick St Clair, letter dated 18th August 1732, quoted by R. W. Ketton-Cremer in Country Neighbourhood, p.87.

'I hope at Christmas, if I live so long, I shall be able to pay most of my debts, and part of my subscription to Cromer Peer. I wish it may stand, and turn to account, but every great sea doth them considerable damage, but that is mostly in the corners, east and west, where the ships come in, and there is a passage for the backwater.'

Patrick St Clair, letter dated 19th August 1732, quoted by R.W. Ketton-Cremer in Country Neighbourhood, p.81. St Clair seems to be describing something more complicated than Philip Vicary's conjectural reconstruction or the existing remains near the pier groyne.

On 22nd September 1732 'there was a very high spring tide, which did bring a heap of stones and sand almost as big as my house into the bason and fill'd up quite the north west passage, so that many people gave the project over for lost; but they have begun to sett down their timbers, and have removed all the stones that lay in their way to the laying down their frames of wood, and I hope they will secure it for this winter.'

Patrick St Clair, letter dated 30th September 1732, quoted by R. W. Ketton-Cremer, Country Neighbourhood, p.89.

Photo of beach remains (Philip Vicary). The stumps of piles extending outwards from the shore are all that remains of the much-repaired jetty breakwater; but what are those at a 45° angle? Described on the 1845 plans as a 'groyne', they could date from the 1730s pier, or even from an earlier one.

1735

A document of 19th April 1735 confirms the agreement of Richard Ellis to allow a dozen signatories to 'have free liberty to Erect a Coy (for their own use only) on the sea shore to the westward of the Pier head in Cromer'. [Lobster coys were wooden cages in the shallow part of the sea, in which lobsters could be kept alive until wanted.] The signatories were also to have 'free liberty to land and lay their several boats on the Banc to the westward of the

Bason (but not to ride in the Bason)'. For this right each man was to pay Richard Ellis two shillings and sixpence a year and was also to do three days' work each year 'at such time and place as the s^d Ri. Ellis shall apoint. This agreement to continue in force for three years, and to comence from Midsumer last.'

Rye, Cromer Past and Present, pp.72-73. It looks as though the 'bason' may have been the harbour basin formed within the new jetty, and perhaps the three days' work was to be done to keep the jetty in good repair. It was a losing battle, however. There are records of bad storm damage in nearby Cley in 1735 and 1741 (see Hooton, The Glaven Ports, pp.166-167), and Ballard's map of 1747 shows no pier at all, despite showing in some detail houses and hedges and even the gun battery at the end of Jetty Street. A deed of 28th August 1765 between Charles Stokes of Stamford and Elizabeth Ellis of Northrepps refers to the deed of 1731, but fails to make it clear whether anything much survived of the pier of 1732.

1781

'There is now no harbour at Cromer.'

History and Antiquities of the County of Norfolk, vol.3, p.36. This seems definite enough, but it may simply mean there is no natural harbour; compare the following extract.

1791

'Cromer . . . has a harbour . . . Ships trading to and from Cromer. - The Blakeney, Sharman, Greenland-man; the Center, Barrell; Cromer, Pank; Experiment, Cook; Van, Ransome; Delme and Gerard, Ransome, jun. and Experience, Cozens; all in the corn and coal trade.'

Universal British Directory, p.598. Here it seems that there is some sort of harbour (if only the shelter afforded by whatever was left of the 1731 pier),

but William Windham describes a ship unloading its cargo in 1790 not at the pier but on the beach. He is surprised, but apparently by the ship being Norwegian rather than by where it was unloaded (Diary , p.205).

An illustration by William Collins (Cromer Museum). The old jetty is no longer being used by ships, for the *Excursions in the County of Norfolk* (1818) confirms that Cromer has 'no harbour' and gives a description of the ships unloading their cargoes on the beach (vol.i, pp.134-135).

1820

This jetty 'was swept away March, 1820'.

Walcott, The East Coast of England, p.101. Newspapers report much storm damage along the Norfolk coast during the early part of the month.

A drawing titled 'Wreck of the Jetteé' (sic), 1821. (Courtesy Ron Fiske)

The first iron jetty

1821-2

'Cromer, April 19. - On Tuesday last [17th April 1821], the Workmen commenced erecting the New Jetty at this place, which will be finished with all possible expedition; the plan adopted promises to possess great strength, and when completed will have a very handsome appearance. The promenade will be considerably longer than the former one, and will be seated and railed so as to render it much more commodious and pleasant.'

Norfolk Chronicle , 21st April 1821, p.2, col.6. The 'promenade' of course does not mean the walkway along the top of the sea wall - which was built later on - but the jetty itself, which was thus being considered as a place for walking on rather than for ships to use.

'After a good deal of argument, dispute, Committee meetings and opinions of Engineers, we have come to a resolution of erecting a Cast Iron Jetty - the first 30 Yards, however, is to be wood-work, which is just begun, & the Iron is expected every day - It was found impracticable to build any part of it with stone (Pebbles) for we have had such scouring tides that the temporary Jetty has been thrice washed away since Christmas . . . the Subscription for the Jetty amounts to £1030 - Contract for Iron will take £700.'

Simeon Simons, letter to J. Lett Esq., 25th May 1821. Simeon Simons was the schoolmaster at the Free School in Cromer, which at the date of this letter was itself being rebuilt.

'The old Jetty was built in 1822 at a cost of £7,200, 70 yards long. The decking was supported on cast iron brackets, these were cast at Saxthorpe by Mr. Haze. I have seen the old Bell which was used to drive the piles. Some part of the Jetty was planked and filled in with rock stones, this is shown on an old print.'

Savin, Cromer, p.93. The figure of £7,200 is almost certainly a misprint for £1,200 (Rye gives the figure as £1,200, whilst White's directory and Walcott both give £1,400). The Saxthorpe foundry had been established in 1800, and William Hase was also responsible, in the 1820s, for designing and supervising the machinery of the Gunton sawmill, and for significant improvements to Captain Manby's invention of a mortar which would fire a line from the shore to rescue the crews of ships in difficulty (see The Banville Diaries, pp.37-38). The foundry continued (under the name of Ling Brothers) until the middle of the twentieth century.

An etching by G. Pank showing the 1821-2 jetty (Crawford Holden Collection)

The jetty in 1821 (Courtesy of Ron Fiske). The old lighthouse seen here, together with all the cliff on which it stood, has since fallen into the sea.

Another sketch from the early 1820s in the collection of Ron Fiske

`The new built and still unfinish'd Jetty (unfinish'd through lack of money) throws the sea so strongly to its eastern side that even an ordinary neap tide tho' with an offshore wind comes up to the cliff foot - and what the future strength of a spring tide or of a series of such tides impelled by a Gale or Gales northerly may be they appear almost to dread to conjecture.'

Mr Marten's Journal, 17th September 1825

`*Cromer, February 18:* On Tuesday night a heavy gale came in from the North, causing a tremendous tide here yesterday morning and at night, which injured the Jetty and entirely swept away Mr. Simons' subscription rooms, &c.'

Norwich Mercury, 20th February 1836. The 'subscription rooms, &c.' were the Bath House, which was rebuilt in time for the holiday season the same year and still stands today as a hotel and public house.

`Cromer, Aug. 23.
`The Cromer Repository,
`In Aid of the Fund towards the Support of the Wall and Improvements.
`The larger room at the New Inn, where the Repository [*i.e.*, a bring and buy sale] was held (the use of which was given by Mr Tucker), was from twelve to four o'clock crowded to excess with visitors.' Bands played and there were flags up at the Coastguard station and at the Hotel de Paris.
'After the Repository, in the afternoon, and again in the evening, the Jetty, (shorn somewhat "of its fair proportions" since the disastrous high wind and tide in Feb.

'Collier unloading, Cromer, October 31 1822' (Courtesy Ron Fiske)

1836), was thronged with fashionable promenaders. The bands playing all the time. . . . The Victoria Parade (between the Walls and Cliffs) were well attended. At night nearly 120 ladies and gentlemen (the *élite* of the company) repaired to the New Inn Ballroom, where Quadrilles and Waltzes, admirably accompanied by Hewlett's Band, were kept up with great spirit till two o'clock in the morning. . . .
'A "Dutch Fair" was the amusement of the following morning, with some of the remaining articles.'

Norfolk Chronicle, 25th August 1838, p.2, cols.6-7. The New Inn was the original name of Tucker's Hotel, which stood next door to what is now Barclays Bank. 'Edwards' wall', as it was known from the name of the engineer who built it (George Edwards of Lowestoft), seems to have been the first serious attempt to protect the sea front from further erosion and simultaneously provide a promenade, which was of grass.

'In 1838, on the eastern side, a groin about 150 yards in length was laid down, running out from the cliff to the north, and which, aided by a sea-wall there erected, it is expected will prevent the recurrence of a similar catastrophe in that quarter; the security of the cliffs immediately below the town was provided for by a breast-work of stone and flint, with winding approaches to the beach and jetty.'

Lewis, Topographical Dictionary , vol.1, p.730.

1841

'A breakwater has also been raised as a further security to the place, and on the stability of this much necessarily depends. Whilst this continues firm, there is little to be apprehended; if this were swept away, the breastwork which defends the cliff would be but a slight defence.'

'The jetty, which formerly projected about seventy yards into the sea, was erected by subscription at the cost of fourteen hundred pounds, in 1822, after the old one had been destroyed by a furious storm. The high tide which we have just recorded [*i.e.*, the storm of 1836] did considerable injury likewise to the jetty, an injury which has not yet been entirely repaired.'

Sargant, Guide to Cromer, 1841 edition, p. 9. The word 'formerly' suggests that the 1836 storm had reduced the length of the jetty.

1844

A writer in 1844 assessed the contribution the jetty could make to the prevention of coastal erosion. He pointed out that the former jetty had caused sand to build up, albeit too far to the north-west of the town to be of much benefit:
'The jetty erected at the north end of the town caused a large mound of sand to accumulate to the northward of it, presenting an inclined surface towards the sea, and during the intervention of northwesterly gales, indigenous grasses sprang up, and covered the surface nearest the banks; this time, however [*i.e.*, in 1836?], the jetty gave way, and the greater portion of the mound of sand was removed; but still there was sufficient left to convince the inhabitants, had the jetty been erected at the south end of the town, their property would have been saved.'
He also considered that the 1822 jetty had failed to offer protection to the shore to the east, because of its design:

'The platform resting upon piles of huge dimensions in height and diameter, appears to have been one continuous length, from the base of the cliffs to the elevated rock at low water mark. Its considerable altitude above the surface of the beach, its unwieldy structure, from the timbers employed, and above all, its extent towards the sea being limited, accounts for its partial destruction in the storm alluded to. The dashing of the waves against the piles, even in calm weather, gives an impetus to the water at their base, and produces eddies or whirlpools, which prevent sea-beach materials accumulating in the immediate vicinity.

'The inhabitants, however, appear so far to have been aware of this circumstance, that in repairing the jetty, they had recourse to iron stanchions, presenting a flat surface towards the sea; but the same impediment to utility still exists.

'Let us now consider whether a jetty could not be constructed to afford not only a delightful promenade, the necessary appendage to a frequented watering place, but the retention of sea-beach materials, and the consequent elevation of the beach.

'For this purpose let wooden piles of English oak be employed, of requisite length to enter the solid strata beneath the surface of the beach. The extremity for insertion must be protected with a rim of the same material, which ought to project above each pile, so as to leave a cavity sufficiently deep to receive the one end of an iron pillar, about eight or more inches in diameter, if considered necessary; and the length of this iron pillar being determined, its upper part can be readily formed to support the wooden plank constituting the platform of the jetty, to which it can be fastened. Now, if the piles are inserted into the beach in a continuous range towards the sea, leaving a space between each pillar, from two to three feet apart, it may readily be inferred, that the desirable object will be realized, and a permanent good will be obtained.'

Hewitt, Essay on the Encroachment of the German Ocean , pp.43, 72-73.

1845

'CROMER. - During the late gale this town has suffered considerably. About nine o'clock on Sunday evening [26th January], the jetty was seen to part in the middle, with a tremendous crash; the dark mass was distinguishable for a short time only, being soon dispersed by the fury of the sea; the further end soon followed, and about nine feet is the only portion left. The floating timber contributed to the destruction of the wood steps leading down to the beach, which are all broken off. The boarding of breakwaters recently erected at great expense has shared a similar fate to the jetty. This has been the highest tide known for the last nine years, and after destroying breakwaters and jetty, washed away the protecting wall, with large portions of the cliff. . . . The cliffs were lined with spectators, some of whom remained until a late hour. Many of the inhabitants did not retire to rest at all, but were engaged in saving all they could of the floating wreck of jetty and breakwaters. The shore next morning exhibited sad tokens of the fury of the sea; the cast iron supports and brows of the jetty being snapped similarly to a tobacco pipe: fragments of the jetty lying in confusion, with masses of wall, and a very large quantity of stones used in the building, are very conspicuous.'

Norfolk News, 1st February 1845, p.3, col.6.

'On Sunday evening last [26th January] a high tide took place here, which was scarcely less disastrous in its effects than the memorable tide of February, 1836. The damage has been immense. The whole of the jetty has been swept away, except a small portion next the cliff, built about seven years ago. . . . The wreck of the jetty is strewed along the beach for many miles, the ponderous iron frames only remaining, which lie huddled together in pieces where they fell, presenting an extraordinary proof of the force of the waves, scarcely one of them remaining whole. . . . It was, we believe, in contemplation some time ago to erect a new jetty according to plans submitted by an eminent engineer; and we hope soon to see a magnificent structure, corresponding with the well-known celebrity of Cromer as a watering place.'

Norwich Mercury, 1st February 1845, p.3, col.7, based on a report sent in by Simeon Simons, proprietor of the Bath House in Cromer. The materials of the old jetty lay on the beach until August, when Henry Sandford was instructed to auction them.

The last wooden jetty

1845

A meeting was held at the Red Lion on 29th January 1845 to decide what was to be done about protecting Cromer from further erosion, and about replacing the jetty. Urgent letters were sent asking various experts whether it would be practicable to get the necessary Act passed before the end of the Parliamentary session.

On 4th February a second meeting was held, this time at the Hotel de Paris. Letters were read from the experts whose advice had been sought, and it was unanimously agreed to apply as soon as possible for an Act 'for the purposes of protecting the Town of Cromer from the encroachment of the sea and for the general improvement of the said Town'. (The latter objective was later dropped.) The original intention was to employ George Edwards as engineer, but Mr Wright was chosen instead; local landowners agreed to underwrite the costs of his surveys, plans, estimates, etc., and his report was received at a public meeting on 24th February.

Minutes of meetings.

'In accordance with a resolution with which I was favoured by Mr Cooch your solicitor on the 13th Inst I have made a survey of the Sea front of the Town of Cromer with a view of adopting some means for the permanent protection of the Cliffs from the further encroachment of the sea, by the erection of sea walls or other works and at the same time so to form them as to be available for walks on Esplanades, and as far as their main object would allow, to forward the general improvement of the Town....

'I beg to submit the plan I propose, to prevent any further destruction of those Cliffs taking place and at the same time by the formation of public Esplanades and walks along the face of the Cliff greatly improve the Town as a place of resort for visitors. . . .

'The Esplanade . . . is to be formed 20 feet in width at the top of the wall, of the same height as that built by Mr Edwards. The wall to be further strengthened by semicircular Buttresses at the angles as described on the Plan accompanying this report, from one of these buttresses I propose a new Jetty upon an improved construction should project of the length and width of the late Jetty; from this point the walls joining that built by Mr Edwards but for a short distance passing in front so as to overlap and protect the part now in danger of being undermined and terminating in a flight of stone steps to the beach. . . .

'In addition to the works above named it will be necessary to erect from three to four Groynes in front of the new wall and probably before Mr Edwards also but the number and situation can only be acertained by actual experiment and watching the effect one or two of them may produce the action of groynes differing greatly even on the same Coast.

'I estimate the Cost of executing the above works including the Jetty to be at a Gross sum of £4870.'

John Wright, letter to the Committee for the Protection of the Town of Cromer, 28th February 1845. The plans were put out to tender in July. Wright's gross figure may include purchase of J. W. Rust's property which was now perched perilously at the top of the cliff and which it would have been impracticable to try and preserve. Rust was willing to sell his property - but wanted £2600 for the whole property, saying he was not interested in selling only part of it. A Mr Barcham was called in from Mundesley (so he was more able to give an independent judgement) and valued the property at £950; eventually, Rust accepted £425 for that part of his property which lay where the new slope was to be constructed; the sum to include the building materials lying below the cliff (which could be used in the new protection works).

An Act of Parliament in 9 Victoria, session 1845, set up the Cromer Protection Commissioners and appointed the first ones, including the big landowners and leading tradesmen. Schedule C to the Act listed the property required for the sea-walls, jetty and sea defences. At their first meeting, on 9th July 1845, the commissioners appointed the local solicitor Robert Cooch as their Clerk; he was to be paid £15 a year. In 1845, he was also paid £966 15s. 1d. for the expenses of getting the Act through Parliament. (He remained Clerk until 1868.)

On 28th July it was resolved 'That the Clerk be instructed to write to Messrs. Clarke and Gooda accepting their Tender at the Two sums amounting to £900 for the erection of the Jetty.'

On 7th August it was 'Resolved that the proposed Jetty shall be placed on the Site of the old one.' (This resolution was, however, rescinded on 13th October.) Wright was to be paid £80 on account, and was to be requested 'to furnish a plan and specification for a Groyne to be erected immediately and in conjunction with the Jetty.' Wright was in despair. It was now five months since he had reported on the work that needed to be done, and although much of the delay was unavoidable (Parliament had first to constitute the Commissioners properly, tenders for the work had to be obtained, and money raised on loan), the Commissioners seemed to be interested only in having their new jetty. They had clearly not understood that simply building a breakwater was not going to stop the sea claiming more land and buildings in the very near future, and they were not even prepared to defer to the engineer's expert opinion on the siting of the jetty. On 10th August Wright wrote to the Commissioners 'declining to act any further as Engineer'.

Although there was a proposal at their next meeting (15th August) to accept Wright's resignation, most of the Commissioners

Signatures of the Protection Commisioners, from the minutes of their first meeting. (See p.28 for a list of the names.) Sir Edward Buxton was absent from this meeting and signed the formal declaration at a later date.

Edwards' sea wall of 1836-8 was the first effective protection of Cromer from costal erosion. The narrow promenade was of grass. Wright's wall of 1846 overlapped this wall at the left hand edge of this picture. (Poppyland Collection)

The Engineers
John Wright

Brought in by the newly formed protection committee in 1845 to save Cromer from the sea.

Born 1799 in Walworth.

Joined the Institution of Civil Engineers in 1830 as an associate and transferred to membership in 1840.

Worked on sea defences in Brighton in the 1830s before moving to Dover, where a sea wall and groynes were being built in preparation for the extension of the main railway line from Folkestone to Dover harbour. When Cromer employed him he was based in Park Lane, London.

Wright designed the first sea wall to protect the western half of Cromer (from Jetty Street to what later became the Melbourne Hotel). To him, the new jetty was simply a minor addition to his sea wall.

When he finished at Cromer he went on to work on the North Holland Canal.

The latter part of his life was spent in Rochester, where he lived first at Upnor Castle House, then on the Esplanade, and by 1877 at Boley Hill, a very exclusive area close to the cathedral.

ANNO OCTAVO & NONO

VICTORIÆ REGINÆ.

****

Cap. xx.

An Act to authorize the Erection of Sea Walls and Works, and a Jetty, at the Town or Parish of *Cromer* in the County of *Norfolk*, and otherwise to provide for protecting the said Town and Parish from the further Encroachment of the Sea.

[30th *June* 1845.]

WHEREAS the Sea Walls and Defences and Works erected for the Protection of the Town and Parish of *Cromer* in the County of *Norfolk* from the Action of the Sea have recently been in great Part destroyed by a Storm, and thereby the Foundations of several Houses and Buildings were undermined, and the Jetty on the Beach was destroyed and washed away, and the Cliffs upon which the said Town is built are exposed to imminent Danger from the Action of the Sea upon them; and it is therefore indispensable, for the Safety of the said Town and Parish, that sufficient Sea Walls, Groins, Jetty, and other Works should be without Delay constructed, for protecting the said Town and Parish from the further Encroachment of the Sea; and it would also tend to the Safety and Security of the said Town and Parish if Powers were granted for the future Maintenance, and for the Alteration, rebuilding, Extension, and Improvement of all existing Sea Walls, Groins, and other Works and Sea Defences in the said Parish; and it would be advantageous

[*Local.*]   6 F   to

Facsimile of the opening pages of the Act of Parliament of 1845

to the Inhabitants of the said Town and the Public resorting thereto if proper and convenient Walks or Promenades on or along such Works were authorized to be made; and it is expedient that Powers should be granted for the Purchase of Houses, Buildings, and Land for the Purposes aforesaid, and for levying Rates for defraying the Expences of carrying into execution the Purposes aforesaid: May it therefore please Your Majesty that it may be enacted; and be it enacted by the Queen's most Excellent Majesty, by and with the Advice and Consent of the Lords Spiritual and Temporal, and Commons, in this present Parliament assembled, and by the Authority of the

Commissioners. same, That the Reverend *William Sharpe*, Vicar of *Cromer*, and the Vicar of *Cromer* for the Time being, the Reverend *Frederick Fitch*, the Licensed Curate under the said Vicar, and the Licensed Curate under such Vicar for the Time being, the Churchwardens of the said Parish for the Time being, the Right Honourable *William* Earl of *Listowel*, *Robert Barclay* Esquire, *Henry Baring* Esquire, *Henry Birkbeck* Esquire, *John Bolding*, *Thomas Boulter*, *John Breese*, Sir *Edward North Buxton* Baronet, *Jeremiah Cross*, *Charles Earle* Surgeon, *Harvey Goodwin* Esquire, *Robert Herring* Esquire, *John Gurney Hoare* Esquire, *Herbert Jarrett Johnson* Gentleman, *Ellis Newstead*, *Matthew Bayfield Ransom*, *John William Rust*, *Henry Sandford*, *Edward Seppings*, and *William Howe Windham* Esquire, shall be the First Commissioners for carrying this Act into execution, and shall continue in Office until the Second *Wednesday* in the Month of *May* One thousand eight hundred and forty-six, or until other Commissioners shall be elected in their Place, in manner herein-after mentioned.

Qualification of future Commissioners. II. And be it enacted, That every Commissioner to be elected as herein-after mentioned under this Act shall be seised or possessed or in the Enjoyment of the Rents and Profits of Lands, Tenements, and Hereditaments within the said Parish of *Cromer*, for an Estate not less than a Life in being for his own Use, rated to the Rate made for the Relief of the Poor of the said Parish in the annual Sum of Twenty-five Pounds or upwards.

No Bankrupt or Insolvent to be a Commissioner. III. And be it enacted, That no Bankrupt or Insolvent, or Person to be elected as herein-after mentioned, not qualified as herein-before mentioned, shall be capable of being or continuing a Commissioner.

No Person holding Office or concerned in a Contract to be a Commissioner. IV. And be it enacted, That if at any Time subsequently to the Appointment or Election of any Commissioner he shall accept or continue to hold any Office or Place of Trust or Profit under this Act, or be interested or concerned in any Contract, or participate in any Manner in any Work to be done or Materials to be supplied under the Authority of this Act, such Person shall cease to be a Commissioner, and his Office shall thereupon become vacant.

Commissioner not incapable of acting as a Justice. V. And be it enacted, That no Person shall be incapable of acting as a Justice of the Peace in any Matter relating to the Execution of this Act by reason of his being a Commissioner.

VI. And

realised that this was not an option they could seriously entertain. They asked him to come to Cromer - though they hedged their bets by asking Mr Sandford (on 9th September) 'to provide materials for and proceed immediately to construct upon such spot of ground as he shall consider most for the general benefit and protection of the Town and in such manner as he shall deem expedient, a Breakwater and that he also proceed in the same manner to lengthen the present Breakwater in front of Mrs. Hogg's house. The whole management of the above matters to be entirely at his discretion.'

Commissioners' minutes. The Melbourne Hotel was later built on the site of Celia Hogg's boarding house.

On 15th September, John Wright attended a meeting of the Commissioners and gave them his report:

'Gentlemen

'I have this morning again inspected the state of the Cliff in front of the Town, and regret to find that from the want of any effectual protection being carried out the injury done to the Cliff very much increased and the danger most imminent. It is much to be lamented that means cannot be found for the erection of the wall as proposed by the plan I had formerly the honour to submit, because I am confident that until that measure be carried out, no effectual or permanent security will be afforded. I would therefore most strongly advise that no more be done in the way of temporary protection (that does not in some way form a part of that plan) than can possibly be avoided.

'The Step most advisable to be taken in the present posture of affairs I think would be to put down a Groyne or breakwater on the Site intended for the new Jetty as shown in the Plan, where it was originally my intention that a Groyne should be erected.

'I certainly would not advise the expenditure of money upon the erection of the Jetty at the present moment - the great and important work for the security of the Town being the Wall, all possible endeavours in the obtaining and husbanding the means should be for that object in the first place.

'I would however now recommend that the Groyne opposite Mrs. Hogg's should be lengthened and repaired and that the working of it be constantly watched, and the planking from time to time be taken off or added as the prevailing wind may render necessary; that it never be allowed to stop any Beach coming from the westward, but only to hold that which may be brought by an Easterly wind.

'I think that under the care and management of Mr. Sandford, if he undertake the office, the Commissioners would be enabled to erect these works themselves without the employment of Contractors - the means of the Commissioners being such that every trifling saving is of importance.'

Commissioners' minutes. The Commissioners really had no choice. They accepted the engineer's report and deferred the jetty, offering to reimburse Messrs Clarke & Gooda for their time and travelling expenses. Raising the money must still have been a problem, for there were yet more delays, but even Mr Sandford became alarmed when November's high tides inflicted further damage on the jetty approaches, and construction of the new sea wall was put out to tender in December.

In December, the Commissioners were told that sixty-five feet of woodwork at the foot of the west cliff had been 'rendered useless by the Storm which took place on the night of the Eleventh instant.'

1846

'The new jetty is to be erected by Messrs. Witting and Smith, of Cromer, for £985. . . . The new break-water, lately built on the site of the old jetty, has caused a great accumulation of beach westward of it, and a corresponding depression on the other side, thereby endangering the safety of the existing wall and esplanade; to counteract the effects of which, other works are now in progress. A difference of opinion exists as to the proper place for the new jetty, some of the Commissioners contending that it must of necessity be on the spot marked out by the engineer, namely, about 30 yards westward of the old one; others, and, we believe also, most of those persons interested in the lodging-houses, who ought to be the best judges, think it should be erected opposite to Tucker's Hotel, which is nearly in the centre of the sea-frontage, and also within the limits of deviation allowed by the Act of Parliament. We wonder that there can be two opinions about it - because, setting aside all other considerations, we are quite sure that a jetty built upon a high sandy beach, and consequently hardly reached by ordinary tides, would not be half so attractive to promenaders during the bathing season as one built on a part of the beach low enough to allow, as formerly, the uninterrupted flow of the sea, at high water, along the greater part of its length.'

Norwich Mercury, 14th March 1846, p.3, col.7. James Witting was a carpenter and joiner who lived in Pump Street (now Chapel Street) and Louden Lane; Thomas Smith was also a joiner in Pump Street. The 'other works' which were under way to prevent Edwards's wall being undermined by the sea involved raising the height of the eastern groyne by at least four feet. The agreed price for the jetty was actually £995 plus scheduled extras. The Commissioners at their meeting of 5th March had also contracted with Jeremiah Wright and George Cattermoul to build the new sea wall, at a cost of £2,323 plus scheduled extras. Crawford Holden gives the total cost of the jetty and promenade as £6,000; Walcott gives it as £10,000.

The first stone was laid by the Vicar on 21st April 1846, and on the same day the first pile was driven.

Mackie, Norfolk Annals.

'It is the general wish of the Commissioners, and the Inhabitants of Cromer, that Wooden Railing be substituted for the Iron Railing originally designed by the Engineer for the Jetty; and that a request be made to him, or Mr Hodges [his representative in Cromer], to furnish with as little delay as possible, the necessary working Plans and Specifications for erecting not only the Wooden Railing but also Seats upon the Jetty.'

Commissioners' minutes, 16th June 1846.

'The new Wall and Jetty are nearly complete.

'At the commencement of driving the Piles for the Jetty, a serious accident happened. My eldest Brother, a master Carpenter, who had the chief management of the Pile driving, had a heavy piece of Iron fall upon him, which crushed the Bones of his thigh in a shocking manner. This brought the work to a stand still - the Contractors being two inexperienced young men. I went down and took the management for them, giving them all my leisure hours by day, & frequently all night. It was very difficult work, as the Piles had to be all driven sloping & within one inch of a straight line all ways.

'The Engineer has pronounced it to be an excellent piece of work.'

Simeon Simons, letter to Goldsmiths' Company, 7th July 1846. He says he is feeling ill, but will probably send an account to the newspaper.

'The new jetty commencing midway between Tucker's Hotel & the Hotel de Paris, extends upwards of 200 feet into the sea, having rails and seats on each side, which to the contemplative and the invalid will be valuable acquisitions. The jetty is 21 feet wide. . . .

'To celebrate the event of throwing the new jetty open to the public, and also to enable the inhabitants and visitors to testify their thanks to the men who had been employed in its construction, it was suggested that the latter should have a dinner given to them on the jetty. . . .

'The table formed of deal plank was placed lengthways of the jetty (covered with a white cloth), so as to form ample room for upwards of 150 persons to dine together. . . . The conveyance of the provisions from the town to the jetty . . . was accomplished by a number of the coast guard service under the command of Capt. Windham, each of whom took a dish of pudding, meat, or potatoes, & descended the cliff in a regular file and in marching order. . . . The guests were supplied with porter, ale, and tobacco. . . . (The toast [to the Queen] was received with acclamation, the guns of the old town battery firing several volleys.'

There followed a rowing match between four white gigs of the coastguard service; then a contest between the Cromer lifeboat and the one from Mundesley - rowing to a vessel moored a mile and a half out, and back again.

'At a later hour in the evening, there was an excellent display of fireworks from the jetty, in which Mr. Coe, of this city, showed very great taste.'

Norwich Mercury, 15th August 1846. The jetty was opened on 7th. This newspaper report, running to well over two thousand words, is presumably from Simeon Simons. The description of the jetty's position is perplexing, for later photographs clearly show it as directly in line with the Hotel de Paris, rather than between there and Tucker's.

1847

On 8th April, tenders are invited 'for puttying the Seats and Railings of the Jetty and painting them with Three Coats of good stone coloured oil paint'. On 19th, a tender of £9.10s. from Mr Neave of Cromer is accepted.
Commissioners' minutes.

1854

'CROMER, 19th Dec.

'The MARSINGALE, [master named] Mutter, from London, in ballast, after losing both anchors, and being very leaky, drifted on shore by Cromer jetty this morning; crew landed: if the weather continues moderate, she may be got off.'
Lloyd's List , 20th December 1854, col.9.

'It being reported to this meeting [7 p.m. on 19th December 1854] that the Brig Marsingale of Whitby had about Two o'Clock this Morning come ashore by the Stone Steps, and carried away a part of the Jetty, and about Twenty Six yards of the Jetty Breakwater

'Moved by Mr. J. W. Rust seconded by Mr. Newstead and Resolved

'That the Breach in the Breakwater be repaired with all possible despatch and that Mr. James Witting and other Carpenters be requested to furnish tenders for the work - the piles and planking and shores short piles braces and wale pieces to be of deal, and the Iron fastenings and all parts of the work to correspond with the remaining part of the Breakwater. Tenders to be furnished to the Commissioners at a Meeting to be held tomorrow Evening at the Clerk's Office at Seven o'Clock to which time and place this meeting be adjourned. (The Piles to be 10 Inches square, and Seventeen Feet long. The small do. 8 inches Square. The Piles to be shod with four fanged shoes not less than 14lb. weight. The Planks to be 3 Inches thick, by Eleven Inches in width.)'

Commissioners' minutes. Two tenders were submitted. Witting's was accepted; the Commissioners resolved on 13th February 1855 to pay him £50 for the repair of the breakwater (though a minority would have preferred him to be paid only £40 on account). Mr Sandford was to auction the wreck of the materials of the jetty and breakwater. The rebuilding of the damaged portion of the jetty itself, however, was not effected until 1860.

1855

On 27th June the Commissioners resolved 'That the Clerk be directed to instruct James Riches forthwith to repair the Stone Steps leading to the Beach, and the Breaches in Edwards's Sea Wall from Simons's Steps [*i.e.*, the ones in front of the Bath House] to the East End of the Wall.' Also, James Witting is to be paid 'the sum of £50 on further account of his Bill for the repair of the Jetty Breakwater and Jetty; and the sum of £4. 11. 3 in discharge of his Bill for Sundries.'

Commissioners' minutes. At the same meeting Thomas Smith had to be replaced as a Commissioner because he was involved in the contract for the 'temporary' repair of the Jetty - another indication that full restoration of the jetty was being deferred. On 26th March 1856, the Commissioners agreed to pay Witting £5 as balance of his bill for repairs of the breakwater, and Newman & Son £10. 16 s. 0 d. for repairing the Stone Steps and coping of the new wall. The breakwater required further extensive repairs in 1857 and again in 1861 and (less extensively) in 1866.

1860

On 19th June the Commissioners resolved 'That it is expedient to restore the Jetty to it's original length, according to the Drawings and Specifications prepared by Mr. Wright the Engineer, with the necessary additions as to drawing the old Piles, the length of the new ones, and the effecting the Junction of the new Work with the old, and that advertisements be inserted in the Norfolk Chronicle and Norwich Mercury for Tenders from persons willing to undertake the work.'

Commissioners' minutes. Smith's tender for £250 was accepted on 5th July.

On 15th October it was resolved 'That Mr. Simeon Simons be requested to survey on behalf of the Commissioners the work lately executed by Mr. Smith in the restoration of the Jetty, and to report to them whether the work has been effected in accordance with the Contract between them and Mr. Smith; and also to report whether it is practicable to bolt the new Piles to the Stumps of the old ones remaining on the Beach.'

Commissioners' minutes. Smith was paid an additional six guineas for the ironwork bracing the new to the old piles. In the following year tenders are invited for painting the jetty (three coats on the new part, one on the old).

1866

In April the Commissioners invited tenders for painting the railings and benches of the jetty, the jetty gangway, and the railings on top of the cliff, with two coats of stone-coloured oil paint. Robert Rogers' tender for £9. 10s. was accepted.

A photo from the 1880s. As well as the jetty, the photograph gives a good picture of the many activities on the beach. (Cromer Museum)

The piers they never built

1866-68

'Order for the Construction, Maintenance, and Regulation of a Pier and Harbour at Cromer, in the County of Norfolk.

'1. The following persons, namely, Henry Peter Andrews, John Hawthorne Lydall, John Bearstall Jerram, . . . are hereby incorporated by the name of "The Cromer Pier Company". . . .

'22. The works authorized comprise the following:- A Pier, Jetty, and Landing Place . . . commencing at a point upon the esplanade or sea wall opposite the end of Jetty Street, thirty-three feet or thereabouts to the east of the existing jetty, and extending thence seawards in a north-north-east direction seven hundred and fifty feet, or thereabouts. . . .'

An attached Schedule gives full details of the maximum tolls which may be levied on ships berthing at the pier, on passengers embarking or disembarking, and on all sorts of goods which may be loaded or unloaded at the pier.

'25. The Company may grant to passengers, promenaders, and other persons, pass tickets. . . .'

Cromer Pier Order, 1867 (30 Vict. c.33).

1883

Plans were drawn up by the Westminster engineers J. F. Puttick and F. H. Cheesewright for 'a pier and landing-place . . . commencing at the point of commencement of the existing jetty or pier, and extending seaward in the same direction as the existing jetty or pier for a distance of 790 feet or thereabouts . . . and the erection of . . . baths, reading, dining, refreshment, and other rooms and erections thereon'.

Plan and Section.

The same plans consist of 'a drawing on waxed linen for a new pier to be constructed at Cromer and dated 27th September 1883. This pier was never actually built but it was going to be a screw pile pier - i.e. the legs of the pier would have ended in huge auger screws and the idea was that these would be rotated and the legs would be driven down into the ground.'

Martin Warren, museum catalogue note. The estimated cost of this pier was £8,700. The plans show that provision was to be made for ships to tie up at the pier head. Screw piles had been used for one of the piers at Brighton, and were to be used in 1896 for the long pier at Bangor.

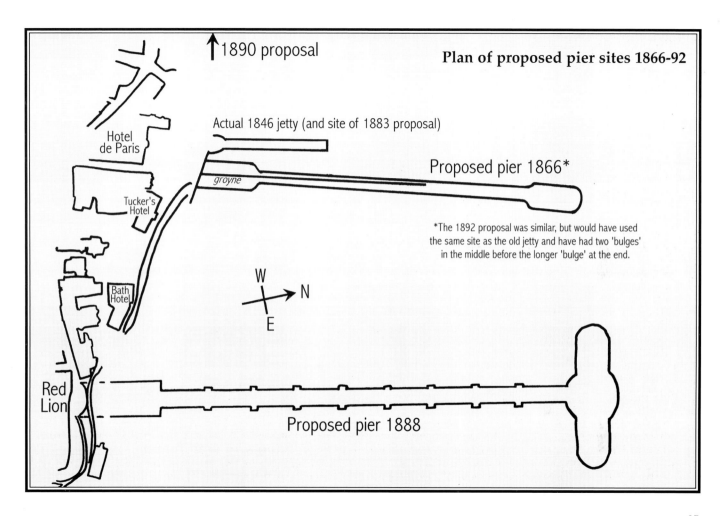

1890 proposal

Plan of proposed pier sites 1866-92

Actual 1846 jetty (and site of 1883 proposal)

Hotel de Paris

Proposed pier 1866*

groyne

Tucker's Hotel

*The 1892 proposal was similar, but would have used the same site as the old jetty and have had two 'bulges' in the middle before the longer 'bulge' at the end.

W

N

Bath Hotel

E

Red Lion

Proposed pier 1888

1888

'At a meeting called for that purpose at the Red Lion Hotel it was said that we should have a Pier as well as a Jetty. The Pier should run out from in front of the Red Lion Hotel, leaving a space between it and the Jetty. The suggested cost was about £25,000. In fact, Mr. Benjamin Bond Cabbell of Cromer Hall, and owner of a great part of Cromer at that time, put up quite large pieces of his land for sale on the West Side in 1890 and again in 1891, and in the Sale books he mentions the fact of a Pier to be erected, as an inducement no doubt.'

Crawford Holden notes.

'Last year the Cromer Esplanade Company were promoting a Bill to enable them to acquire . . . land to carry out certain works, including a promenade, pier, jetty, and landing and shipping place . . . for the accommodation of steam and other vessels, and the embarking and landing of passengers, goods, and merchandise, and also for a promenade and other purposes, such pier commencing at a point on the esplanade at the foot of the cliff opposite and nearly due north of the Red Lion Hotel, and thence extending across the foreshore and into the sea . . . one thousand feet.

'The Bill also provides for an hydraulic or other lift or hoist, and also stairs from the esplanade to the top of the cliff. . . . The undertakers propose from time to time to erect upon or near to the pier a pavilion, saloon, assembly or music-room, with reading, refreshment, and other rooms, shops, bazaars, baths, and other conveniences. The pier will be constructed on iron or wooden piles, so that the free use of the shore under the pier shall be in no way restricted. When this spirited enterprise shall have been carried out Cromer will have an additional charm for many, and there will be provided what numbers desire, a pleasant place of resort in the evening.'

Knights, Illustrated Guide, pp.29-30. Plans had been drawn up by the London engineers G. B. Nichols & Son and George B. Jerram. The Commissioners consistently opposed the Red Lion site, on the grounds that in such a position it would overlook the chief bathing place and would hence affect the prosperity of Cromer. The Chief Inspector of the Lifeboat Institution had also pointed out to them that it would, 'with certain winds, add materially to the difficulties and danger of launching' the lifeboat from the bottom of the Gangway. By July 1890 the promoters had failed to raise the necessary capital, so they applied to the Board of Trade for a year's extension of the original two-year Order. It was now intended to construct the pier opposite the Prince of Wales Road, leaving headroom of 18 feet over the esplanade; by the beginning of September it was being stated that 'the new pier would be commenced shortly, and this would be as nearly as possible opposite the Grand Hotel now in course of erection' (Norfolk Daily Standard, 4th September 1890, p.3).

'In the centre of the Pier will stand a handsome pavilion, containing reading, retiring, and refreshment-rooms, &c. The measurements of this pavilion are 100 ft. by 60 ft., with a height of 30 ft. from the floor to the pitch of the roof. It is to be constructed of wood, with a zinc roof, and will be very ornamental in design.

'Mr Nichols [the architect, who was also about to begin a pier at Milford Haven] was very sanguine as to the success of the under-taking. . . . It would be commenced as soon as possible contingent upon the delay necessitated by the alterations to the plan owing to removal of the site. . . . "We shall certainly begin building within the year. . . . When the Pier is built, we shall be able, at all times, to land passengers or merchandise at low water. . . ." Its attractions, when it comes into existence, should at once quadruple the number of visitors.'

Norfolk Daily Standard, 25th July 1890, p.8.

The Cromer Esplanade Pier Company was registered in February 1888 for the purpose of constructing this pier and esplanade, 'but operations were never commenced, although, when in January, 1891, they were contemplated, it was considered advisable to re-register the company. The capital of the company was agreed at £25,000, but there was no prospectus, and the only shares issued were one £5 share to each of the signatories to the memorandum of association. . . . The only other asset [by April 1892] was a sum of £1,000, being the value put upon the Board of Trade's concession with rights to build the pier, etc.' Once this had expired, 'the assets practically disappeared, and the Official Receiver could hold out no hope of the payment of a dividend to the creditors.' Mr Jerrom, the engineer, claimed £734 for his services, but the Official Receiver was left to act as liquidator and wind up the company.

The Times, Bankruptcy Court report, 8th April 1892, p.14, col.3. In the previous week the paper had referred to 'assets of £950 and liabilities of £1438', and said that 'the insolvency is attributable to the want of capital to carry out the undertaking' (2nd April, p.16, col.5). An Order for the compulsory winding up of the company had been issued on 30th January, on a creditor's petition (The Times, 1st February 1892, p.3, col.1).

1892

The Protection Commissioners themselves 'Resolved that Sir John Coode be requested to prepare a Plan for the further and better protection from the sea of the whole of the sea front of Cromer'. The plan his partnership came up with involved building several new groynes, and extending in timber the existing concrete groyne on the East beach; a pier on the same site as the existing jetty would have been similar to the one which was in fact opened in 1901, but a little longer.

Commissioners' minutes, 2nd December 1891; Cromer sea protection - proposed foreshore improvements.

It was not universally agreed that a pleasure pier was a good thing: a description of Cromer in 1892 states that 'there are (as yet) no conventional abominations; no "parade," no villainous structure called a pier sticking aimlessly into the sea with a band-stand and performing fleas; only a homely little "jetty" and a sufficient stretch of sand below.'

Article in the St. James's Gazette , 18th May 1892, reprinted in Holiday Notes, 1894, p.5.

1890

'The Jetty . . . has recently undergone considerable repair, the three outer tiers of wooden piles having been replaced by iron ones, strengthened by stays. The cost of the work is about £270. Mr C. T. Dennis, of Lynn, was the contractor, and the work was carried out from the plans and under the superintendence of Mr Alfred Dodman.'

Norfolk Daily Standard, 18th March 1890, p.4. It was as early as 6th February 1889 that the Commissioners had appointed a committee to inspect the jetty and report on the best means of repairing it. On 26th June 1889 they decided to replace the last three rows of four piles each with nine iron screw piles. The ironwork was fixed between December and February, and on 7th May 1890 the Commissioners ordered the jetty deck to be repaired.

'Safe above any possible sea the Jetty may, doubtless, appear to be to visitors; but the furious waves at stormy periods dash completely over it, sometimes starting its timbers and wrecking its railings.'
Knights, Illustrated Guide, p.34.

The jetty in 1895 (Crawford Holden Collection)

1897

'At Cromer [on 30th November], 30 feet of the far end of the jetty were washed away, the approach wall was damaged, and the near end of the jetty lifted out of position. . . . There was a renewal of the gale on Wednesday night, and in the early hours of Thursday [2nd December] the ketch Hero, of Goole, with coal, came ashore about 100 yards to the west of the crippled jetty.'

Norfolk Chronicle, 4th December 1897, p.8, col.5. This storm claimed at least thirty lives around the Norfolk coast, and seven other ships were reported wrecked. Assertions that the Hero collided with the jetty cannot be substantiated by newspaper reports or lifeboat records.

'The storm may be said to have begun about five o'clock on Sunday afternoon [28th November]. . . . Between 9 and 11 the seas were running very high. . . . The Cromer Jetty suffered severely. A number of its iron stays were washed away, and this favourite marine promenade left but a wreck of its former self. It looks more like a dismantled schooner with sea-swept deck than the once compact and sound little structure that for long has been the sport of storms. For the many sightseers who thronged the cliffs above, and viewed from safe vantage ground the work of destruction below, the scene was one not soon erased from memory. Even

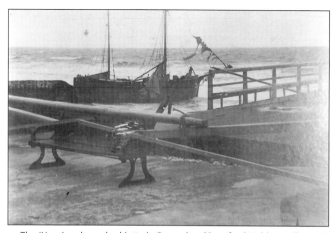

The 'Hero' and smashed jetty in December (Crawford Holden Collection)

from their high position they were not free from the spray of the angry billows.'

Eastern Daily Press, 30th November 1897, p.5, col.6. The following day the Commissioners deputed their Works Committee to examine the jetty and report back; one week later, with a report detailing not only storm damage but also a great deal of rotten timber, they agreed to take down the rest of the jetty.

`Mr. W. G. Sandford, under instructions from the Protection Commissioners, offered the Jetty for sale by public auction. Much interest was taken in the proceedings, which were, however, of very brief duration. The structure was offered in one lot, and under the conditions of sale the purchaser is obliged, under penalty, to have it removed by the end of January. Another condition is that the piles are to be cut off 4 feet below the present level of the Beach. Bidding began at £2, and the hammer went down at £40, the purchaser being a Mr. Isaacs.'

The auction of the old jetty. Auctioneer W. G. Sandford is standing beneath the bandstand which in the future 1890's formed part of the slope in front of the Hotel de Paris. (Crawford Holden Collection)

Unidentified newspaper cutting. J. J. Isaac was a builder from Yarmouth. On 5th January 1898 his solicitor wrote to the Commissioners suggesting they reconsider the question of repairing and extending the old structure ('my Client is used to pier work, and could be quite willing...'). The Commissioners declined the offer.

'The jetty was badly damaged in a storm. . . .
'A ladies' fashion is said to have played a part in this disaster. Originally, the decking of the pier consisted of wooden planks carefully spaced breadthwise, to allow the waves to spill harmlessly through when the seas were rough. But around 1897 came a fashion for slim stiletto heels. Complaints from the ladies that their heels were wont to catch in the planking with dire results (wilful and indecent exposure perhaps?) persuaded the Foreshore Protection Commissioners to a piece of foolish chivalry: the laying of more planks, lengthwise, leaving no gaps. In the next strong gale the unbroken flooring offered too much resistance and was ripped up in solid pieces, dragging many of the supporting piles right out of the sea.

'The way was now clear for a new construction combining the functions of the vanished jetty and the projected pleasure pier. There was still some discussion about the best location, and it may well be significant, as the site eventually chosen was immediately below the Hotel de Paris, that the owner of this hotel was also Chairman of the Protection Commissioners who made the final decision.'

Lockwood, Part III, Norfolk Fair, January 1976, p.10. It has to be said that a search of the Protection Commissioners' minutes and accounts has failed to find any reference to the double planking of the jetty, nor is it to be seen in any photographs. In any event the mistake with the decking, if it was ever made, was not repeated: the new pier featured a splash deck, a section just behind the entrance gates which was left unfixed so that it would lift when high waves rose through the lattice supports.

'The gale has done what the powers that be failed to accomplish. The Jetty is doomed, and it has brought the town face to face with the necessity of having a pier. There have been attempts already to float a company to carry out the project, but the Commissioners have been so anxious to have a finger in the pie and yet be absolved from all financial responsibilities that the promoters became so disgusted at the manner in which their overtures were received, no wonder they failed to agree to the clauses which the body referred to wished to have inserted in the Act.'

Cromer & North Walsham Post, 4th December 1897, p.5, col.2.

The poster for the auction of the materials from the jetty.
(Cromer Museum)

40

The present pier

Construction

On 3rd August 1898 the Protection Commissioners decided to apply to other seaside towns for information about engineers employed on the construction of piers. On 23rd August they appointed W. T. Douglass, who was to be paid 5% of the cost of whatever works were carried out, with a single payment of 100 guineas for consultancy and expenses if the project did not proceed.

Commissioners' minutes.

A committee was appointed to visit other seaside places, and they recommended:
`That the kiosks adopted be similar to those at Margate or Dover, but with roofing like Ventnor Pavilion.
`That the shelters be similar to those on Ventnor Pier, but with a few alterations, and that provision be made for closing the ends with revolving shutters, similar to the band shutters at Margate, or other suitable method.
`That the flooring of the pier be similar to Ventnor, and laid lengthways, one-quarter inch apart, the portion next the retaining wall to be wood lattice work, similar to that at Herne Bay.
`That the gates be similar to those at Dover.
`That the sloping approaches be divided by balustrades similar to that at Shanklin, but slightly heavier and turned, instead of square.
`That the sloping approaches and steps between same be paved with materials similar to the finer pavement at Southsea.
`That provision be made to fix a canvas awning the whole length on either side of the pier as a shield from the wind when necessary. . . .

`That lamps be fixed both sides of the pier at 15 to 20 yards apart, similar to Ventnor.
`Since visiting the various piers the committee are most strongly of opinion that the interests of the town would be best served by retaining the entire control of the pier and not by having it controlled by a public or private company.' The committee noted that `where piers were in the hand of companies they were badly kept, and advertisements covered everything'. In contrast, the Commissioners `were studying the interests of the town in keeping the pier in their own hands'. Optimistically, some of the Commissioners `did not believe the pier would cost the town one farthing in the end'. Realistically, the clerk worked out that the revenue from the pier might cover one third to one half of the rate which would be needed to build it.
`The Chairman said they could not expect the pier would pay the same as those on the south coast, where the bulk of the profits was derived from people landing from passenger steamers. The landings at their pier would be very few - possibly a few from Yarmouth. Then, their pier was actually at a corner of the coast, where the tides ran strongly, and in case of a wreck it would smash the structure. They stood at great risk.'
One Commissioner asked, `I take it that we can insure against that risk?'
He was told, `We must have a pier, there is no doubt.'
Unidentified newspaper report of 5th November 1898.

The bill to go before Parliament was to provide for a pier not more than 500 feet long, designed with a view to future extension; the strengthening of the existing sea wall and its extension both to the east and as far as the westward boundary of the parish; and a new east groyne. A special meeting of the Commissioners was held on 7th December to study the draft Bill and to rescind any previous resolutions or instructions which might conflict with it.

The Cromer Protection Bill 1899 was introduced in the House of Lords on 14th February 1899 and passed all stages without debate, receiving the Royal Assent on 9th August.

Commissioners' minutes; Parliamentary Debates (1899), vol. 76.

'Messrs. Douglass & Arnott of Westminster were the engineers. Mr. Alfred Thorne was contractor for the Pier. . . .'

The structure is 500 ft. long. . . . It is constructed of wrought-iron piles, surmounted by cast-iron columns, with steel lattice girders supporting the deck. The piles rest 20 ft. down on the bed of the sea, and the first was driven on 13th January last year. . . .'

Eastern Daily Press, 8th June 1901, p.5, col.8. Thorne, a member of a well known Greenock family, had an office in Victoria Street, Westminster, and had worked with John James Webster, a Victoria Street engineer, on Dover pier in 1893 and Bangor pier in 1896. Adamson (Seaside Piers, p.106) describes the design as 'short and wide, with a consequently high earning potential and low maintenance costs'. The cost of construction was £17,067. 14s. 5d. , the Protection Commissioners borrowing money from the Alliance Assurance Co. at 4% over sixty years.

'The Foreshore occupied by the pillars and supports of the Pier is held from the Crown in perpetuity subject to a rent of 1/- per annum if demanded.'

Valuation Office fieldbook. The Board of Trade had granted these rights on 1st June 1900.

The Engineers
William Tregarthen Douglass

Designed Cromer's present pier and sea wall.

Born 1857; educated at Dulwich College and served a pupilage under his father (who was Engineer to Trinity House).

Lived in Campden Hill, Kensington.

Designed lighthouses all over the world and was joint author of the article on them in the great eleventh edition of the *Encyclopaedia Britannica*. Also an authority on coastal erosion, foreshore protection and the travel of beaches.

Became Inspecting Engineer to the Royal National Lifeboat Institution in 1888, and was consultant to various lighthouse and harbour authorities.

Chosen by Cromer Protection Commissioners from a shortlist of four on 23rd August 1898.

Also responsible for work on Eugenius Birch's pier at Margate, and for sea defence works at Sheringham, Lowestoft and elsewhere.

Drowned in 1913 when sailing near Start Point in a friend's small boat.

The pier under construction in 1900 (Cromer Museum)

1901

'The splendid new pier at Cromer was opened today with becoming ceremonial. Lord Claud Hamilton unlocked the handsome gates with a gold key at 1.30, and a luncheon followed at the Hotel de Paris. The G.E.R. Company brought down a company of London pressmen, and the M. & G.N.R. another party, who lunched at the Hotel Metropole. Later, the strangers were conveyed round the district, and introduced to the beauties of "Poppyland".'

Norfolk Daily Standard, 8th June 1901. Hamilton was chairman of the Great Eastern Railway Company.

'Lord Claud Hamilton, in proposing "Success to the Cromer Pier and Prosperity to the Town of Cromer," said he had known Cromer personally or by reputation for the past fifty years. . . . He remembered well how his mouth used to water at the accounts by his youthful schoolfellows [members of the Hoare and Buxton families] of the masses of amber and jet they used to pick up on the Beach at Cromer. He hoped to emulate them, but he learned that Cromer at that period of its history was an almost inaccessible spot. He understood that it was entirely inhabited by Gurneys and Buxtons and Hoares and wild parrots. . . .

'Mr. Jarvis in responding, said that . . . they had to obtain a special Act of Parliament which met with opposition from various quarters. Then when the work was begun, the foundations were washed away four times. The sea also smashed the pile-driving engine, and washed away the staging. . . . The Commissioners had embedded in their scheme all the best points of other piers, and carefully excluded everything that would lower the tone of the place. They [the public] would not find any trade advertisements, or automatic machines, or drinking bars, or shops on Cromer Pier. . . .'

Eastern Daily Press, 10th June 1901, p.6, cols.4-6.

The opening day for the new pier. (Crawford Holden Collection)

In October 1907, the Clerk stated that the total cost of construction of pier and shelters was £18,800. A fixed annual charge of £881 for interest and instalment of loan would be payable for several years, in addition to which there would be working expenses and general maintenance charges which, taking the average of the last three years, came to about £480. This gave an annual expenditure of about £1,360 in addition to outlay on the provision of entertainments.

Commissioners' minutes.

'The new Pier, ornamental, and rather alien in appearance, is evidence of Cromer's determination to be select and to stand aloof from popular vulgarities. . . . At Cromer, in fact, the higher vulgarity is cultivated, just as at Yarmouth you plumb the depths of the lower variety. The tripper, holiday-making at Yarmouth, who comes over to see what Cromer is like, and finds no whelk and oyster stalls, and no popular entertainment on the sands, thinks it dull; and the average man, wandering along the Lighthouse cliffs in danger of having an eye knocked out by the wealthy and selfish vulgarians who practise golf there, is prone to consider Cromer a fine place, except for the people who frequent it, and for whose benefit the giant hotels facing the sea have been built, and still are building.'

Harper, The Newmarket . . . and Cromer Road, p.351.

1930

'At Cromer, 57 of the 91 piles were found to be worn and even holed in 1930. Contractors May, Gurney & Co. of Norwich encased the damaged piles in concrete cylinders carried down to the chalk into which the piles were driven. . . . An inspection of the pier by consulting engineers Lewis & Duvivier in the mid-1950s revealed that many of the concrete encasements placed around the piles in 1930 had been undermined and beach movement coupled with abrasion by moving sand and shingle meant they no longer rested on chalk. Underpinning was carried out in 1955 and in 1968.'

Adamson, Seaside Piers, pp.74-75. Some of these piles were badly damaged in a storm in January 1976, and resleeving was carried out in April/May of that year.

World War 2
1940

On the outbreak of war in September 1939, the pier was at once closed. 'Not only was the pier closed but the decision made, in July 1940, to blow up a central portion to prevent any invading troops having easy access to the town. Local people were warned that the demolition would take place at 12 noon on a particular Sunday and advised to open their windows to lessen any danger from blast. As the hours went by and nothing happened many closed their windows, only to regret it when at about 4 o'clock there was an almighty explosion, blast and debris shattering windows and damaging property and a large piece of metal girder landing in Church Street opposite Woolworths store. Fortunately no-one was injured. However, having achieved the aim of the exercise it was then realised that the lifeboat crew could not get down to the lifeboat house so temporary planking was put over the hole - and it is not disputed that in dark and wet conditions members of the lifeboat crew were probably in greater danger going across the gap than they were out at sea!'

Brooks, Coastal Towns at War, pp.10-11.

Postwar development
1946

'Cromer pier . . . has been acquired by the Hunstanton Pier Company. . . .

'An offer had been made by the Hunstanton Pier Company to take over the war damage claim, put the pier in order by next season, have the use of it rent free for a number of years, and afterwards arrange a lease.'

Eastern Daily Press, 25th Sep 1946. In the event, the offer was not taken up.

1947

The Wigan Construction Company's tender for reconstruction was accepted in May.

A picture by H.H.Tansley, taken in 1947, showing the repairing of the middle section of the pier after the war. (Courtesy Peter Brooks)

1948

An Act of Parliament dissolved the Cromer Protection Commisioners as from 1st October 1948 and transferred their property, rights, powers and obligations - including responsibility for the pier - to the Cromer Urban District Council.

Cromer Urban District Council Act 1948. The UDC was succeeded under the local govenment reorganisation of 1974 by the North Nofolk District Council.

1951

'Cromer Pier will be 50 years old on June 9th. The pier will be reopened by H.M. Lieutenant of Norfolk (Sir Edmund Bacon) on that day.'

Eastern Daily Press, 13th January 1951. In this year, steps and a curved wall were built at the pier entrance, 12 feet further out than the existing ones. The work cost £40,000 for the work below deck level, £20,000 for the pavilion, and £30,000 for the associated sea wall repairs.

Concrete slabs lifted by the heavy seas of 1953. (Crawford Holden Collection)

The snapped leg after the 1953 floods.
(Dennis Burns, Crawford Holden Collection)

1953-55

The famous high seas of January caused much damage, strewing theatre seats along the beach and dislodging many of the concrete paving slabs which had replaced the wooden decking. The water rose so high in the lifeboat house that the boat was floated and thrown against the sides of the house, causing severe damage.

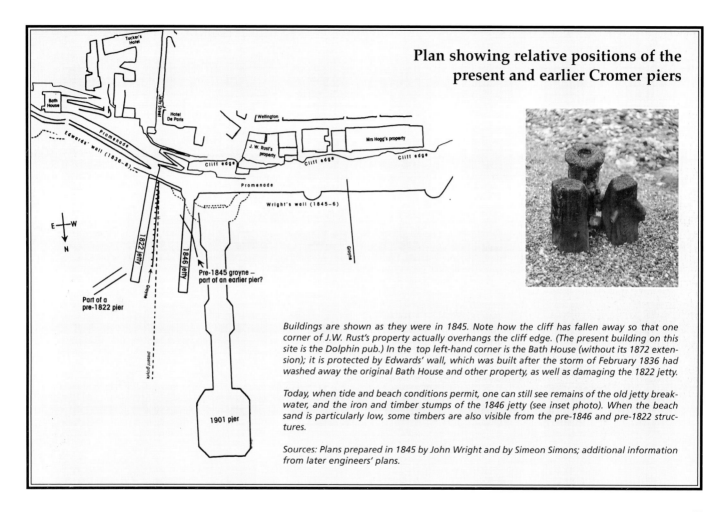

Plan showing relative positions of the present and earlier Cromer piers

Tucker's Hotel

Bath House

Jetty Street

Hotel De Paris

Wellington

Edwards' wall (1836-8)

Promenade

J. W. Rust's property

Cliff edge

Mrs Hogg's property

Cliff edge

Cliff edge

Promenade

Wright's wall (1845-6)

E—W N

1822 jetty

1846 jetty

Groyne

Pre-1845 groyne — part of an earlier pier?

Groyne

Part of a pre-1822 pier

present groyne

1901 pier

Buildings are shown as they were in 1845. Note how the cliff has fallen away so that one corner of J.W. Rust's property actually overhangs the cliff edge. (The present building on this site is the Dolphin pub.) In the top left-hand corner is the Bath House (without its 1872 extension); it is protected by Edwards' wall, which was built after the storm of February 1836 had washed away the original Bath House and other property, as well as damaging the 1822 jetty.

Today, when tide and beach conditions permit, one can still see remains of the old jetty breakwater, and the iron and timber stumps of the 1846 jetty (see inset photo). When the beach sand is particularly low, some timbers are also visible from the pre-1846 and pre-1822 structures.

Sources: Plans prepared in 1845 by John Wright and by Simeon Simons; additional information from later engineers' plans.

'After the storm damage [of January 1953] it was the Council's obvious duty to restore the sea defences first, and this was done. The next problem was to reinstate damaged amenities.

'They were told by their consultants that to restore the substructure of the pier would cost about £23,000, and to restore the pavilion £9000. . . . While the pier restoration was going on, they decided to restore the shops at the pier entrance and the gates.'

Eastern Daily Press, 4th February 1955. The repairs to the substructure were done by Carter-Horseley Ltd. This reconstruction saw the pier through to 1968, when Welding Constructions and Repairs Ltd overhauled the steel piling, which had rust half an inch thick in places. The estimate for these repairs was £27,618, plus a further £8,135 for repairs to the column bases by Dockland Diving Engineering Ltd.

The entrance to the pier after the 1953 floods.
(Dennis Burns, Crawford Holden Collection)

Repairs under way in 1953, with the flat roofed kiosks.
(Dennis Burns, Crawford Holden Collection)

1963

On the August Bank Holiday weekend, a record 11,800 people paid to pass through the turnstiles onto the pier. (The total number for the year 1960 had been over 100,000.)

1974

Ownership of the pier was transferred from the Urban District Council to the new North Norfolk District Council.

1978

In the storm of 11th January, many of the concrete decking slabs were lifted by the sea, and the doors of the lifeboat house smashed.

1990s

Dossor East Civil and Structural Consultants, based in Norwich, were appointed to carry out a full structural survey. The pier was repainted and its steelwork renovated at a cost of half a million pounds. In February 1993, storms damaged the north-west corner and a large area of decking; repairs were carried out under partial closure.

In the mid-1990s the original edging was replaced with new 'fibre' concrete, and the concrete decking was replaced with hardwood timbers.

The Tayjack incident

1993

`No previous storm damage [to the 1901 pier] compared with the event that unfolded on Sunday 14th November, 1993. A jack-up platform, *Tayjack 1*, was being used for the construction of Anglian Water's long sea outfall.' [This was to replace a number of short-er sewage outfall pipes, including one which entered the sea underneath Cromer pier.]

`The platform was working over a mile offshore to the north-west of Cromer.

`During spring tides and strong north westerly gales the platform was overwhelmed. All its four legs sheared off, with cranes, cabins and equipment being dumped into the sea. The platform module, a box measuring 18 metres by 12 metres by 1.5 metres and weighing some 80 tonnes, had broken loose and drifted in towards Cromer. The platform beached to the west of the pier at approximately 4.55 p.m. and by 5. 25 p.m. had cut the pier in two and damaged a total of thirteen groynes (breakwaters).

The Pier from the west after the Tayjack had gone through it from this side.
(Poppyland Photos)

`It was not until the following morning, a mild sunny day, that the full extent of the damage could be seen. Thirty six metres of the inshore end of the pier had been destroyed, marooning the rest of the pier and Cromer's extremely important offshore lifeboat. The damage to the pier was fortunately limited to the breach and the stability of the remainder of the pier had not been adversely affected. There is little doubt that the two year programme of structural refurbishment of the pier, which was within four weeks of completion, prevented the damage from being far more extensive. Besides the physical breach, all water, electricity and telephone links with the pier and RNLI had been destroyed.

`On the night of the incident, North Norfolk's Technical Services staff, supported by the Emergency Services, secured the area of the pier forecourt. These measures were necessary to prevent injury to members of the public. The following day the contractor, John Martin Construction Ltd, began clearing up the mass of twisted and tangled steel and cast iron that littered the beach.

`. . . The gap was far too big to be breached using planks. Allowing the lifeboat crew access and providing access for engineering works became a high priority. On Thursday the 18th November, less than four days after the collision, the breach had been spanned by a temporary wire rope suspension bridge, very bouncy but quite effective. Safe access to the marooned pier had been provided and, very importantly, the lifeboat was back in service.

`The suspension bridge could be considered only a temporary arrangement. Whilst it was perfectly safe to use, it was a little difficult to traverse. Also it was a little fragile and in the way of reconstruction work. A more substantial bridge was needed, sited alongside the breach rather than across it. This was built and open for use, though not by the public, by Christmas. . . .

`Nobody in their right mind would plan to construct a pier or part of a pier from scratch in mid-winter on a coast facing the North Sea. This did not stop North Norfolk District Council's Civil Engineers from getting to grips with the problem. Rather, it heightened the challenge. Within days of the incident, a programme for the pier's reconstruction had been fixed. By Christmas, only five weeks after the collision, detailed drawings were available and tenders for the pier's reconstruction sought.

`On the 25th January, 1994, ten weeks after the collision, work started on site, on the reconstruction of the pier. On the 1st May, 1994, the pier was re-opened to the public by the Rt. Hon. Mrs Gillian Shephard MP, i.e., only fourteen weeks after the site works began.'

Account by Peter Lawton, Technical Services Officer, North Norfolk District Council, in Cromer Town Guide and Trade Directory 1995/96, pp.27-29.

Dossor East designed and detailed the work required to rebuild the pier and designed the rope bridge. John Martin Construction Ltd were the contractors for rebuilding the damaged section, with cast iron columns supplied by Norcast and steelwork by Code Arc.

The pier from the west. The Tayjack ended up against the promenade on the left of the picture. (Poppyland Photos)

The re-opening of the pier took place on a beautiful sunny Sunday morning in May. It attracted perhaps the greatest number of people on the pier at one time that had been seen for many years. (Poppyland Photos)

Crowds gather at the pier entrance ready for the reopening by Gillian Shephard. (Poppyland Photos)

STRUCTURES ON THE PIER

Gates, turnstiles and kiosks

1901

'On either side of the massive entrance gates are turnstiles, artistic kiosks, and smaller exit gates.'

Eastern Daily Press, 8th June 1901, p.5, col.8. The charge for entrance to the pier was 1d. ; in 1906, 2,000 people paid 2d. each to visit the pier on Whit Monday. In 1921 it was decided to charge 4d. for admission to the pier when evening concerts were being played.

1912

'It was Resolved that a thermometer be provided and the temperature of the Sea taken each morning during the Season and posted at the Pier Gates.'

Works Committee minutes, 1st May 1912.

The original iron entrance gates & kiosks (Randall/Salter Magic Lantern Collection)

1951

'Ever since the pier was derequisitioned by the military authorities at the end of the war, work of putting it back into use for holidaymakers has gone on steadily. Last year the pier pavilion was reopened for entertainment. . . . At present contractors are building shops and a new pay box at the entrance to replace the temporary premises which were in use last summer.'

Eastern Daily Press, 13th January 1951. The original cast iron gates had probably gone for scrap during the war. The new entrance structure had a unified, high-pitched, tiled roof, but after the flood damage of 1953 this was replaced by a flat roof. By 1965 the entrance charge was 4d. for adults, 2d. for children. Admission charges were not abolished until 1984.

The entrance after the 1953 floods, showing the pitched roof
(Crawford Holden Collection)

1976

'At the pier entrance there are two shops, one leased to Mr. Bolton for £357.50 plus rates and the other, a cafe, leased to California Catering Ltd., at £460 a year plus rates.

'The council budgets for an annual turnstile income of about £8000, representing 140,540 admissions.'
North Norfolk News, 27th February 1976, p.1.

1989

Pier entrance restyled with domes (reflecting the shape of the Pavilion roof) instead of the former flat roof.

Bandstand

The bandstand in 1901. (Randall/Salter Magic Lantern Collection)

On 4th May 1892 the Commissioners accepted a proposal from Ernest F. Jarvis and F. W. Rogers to supply two or three bands to play three nights a week in the season. (Ernest Jarvis lived in Albert House, next door to the Hotel de Paris and actually overlooking the jetty approach.) In connection with this they also offered to erect 'a small stand in the centre of the circle or approach to the Jetty, to be so arranged as not to interfere with the Commissioners' works, or cause any obstruction, or impede the traffic and could if necessary be used at any time as a place of Shelter.' Maybe this sweetener proved a little too costly for the modest return they got in collections at the concerts, for on 4th October the following year 'Mr E. F. Jarvis asked if the Commissioners were inclined to take over the band stand by purchase.' On 17th August 1895 it was 'Resolved that permission be given to the Fishermen to place seats on either of the Esplanades at such times as the Band plays.'

Commissioners' minutes.

The new pier had an octagonal bandstand, with a tiled roof 26 feet across supported on 4-inch cast iron columns. This appears to have been built to a standard design by David Rowell & Co. Ltd of Clapham Junction.

Undated plan and elevation by David Rowell & Co.

After the conversion of the enclosure into the Pavilion Theatre, bands would play in the afternoons at the centre of the pier, in the open (unless it was raining, in which case they adjourned to the Pavilion). In 1928 'the question of the provision of shelter for the pier Band by the addition of a roof to the existing screen was considered . . . Resolved that the work be proceeded with . . . and that the question of the erection of a Bandstand be considered before next Season.'

Works Committee minutes, 5th July 1928. In 1930, G. T. Woodward & Son of Cromer built a circular bandstand between the central shelters, with a cupola roof to match the entrance kiosks. It survived the destruction of the middle of the pier in the war; possibly it was demolished to make way for the restaurant which was proposed for the site in 1948?

Pavilion
1899

'A letter was received stating that the opposition would be made to the Bill if a pavilion was proposed to be erected on the pier. As a matter of fact, a pavilion was never proposed. . . . Mr Puxley [had] suggested a pavilion at the Commissioners' meeting, but was outvoted. He understood there was opposition to the Bill, and though he was a guarantor he trusted it would be successful, for rather than have a pier with no pavilion he would have no pier at all. . . . Mr Broadhurst . . . said a pavilion on the pier would be most fatal to the highest interests of the town. They would cease to be placed in the same category as Bournemouth and Ventnor if they proceeded to go in for popular entertainments of the character indicated for the Pier.'

Cromer and North Walsham Post, 14th January 1899. In the event, the respected Ventnor looked with admiration on the Cromer pier (Isle of Wight Advertiser, 15th June 1901), though at this period there was no pavilion upon it.

1905-

On 5th October 1904 the Commissioners approved Douglass & Arnott's plans for roofing over the shelter at the head of the pier to form a pavilion. The alterations were carried out in 1905 by Boulton & Paul of Norwich, at a cost of £1,800, and the original canvas awning was offered for sale. The inside of the pavilion was painted a dead white with a grey dado for the columns. The bandstand was later replaced by a proper stage with a proscenium arch, and in 1912 matchboarding was placed over the stage to form a ceiling. There were several purchases of tip-up seats between 1911 and 1928 - evidently the old chairs were only being replaced piecemeal; it was still being resolved as late as July 1923 that cushions should be provided for the back rows of the second reserved seats. Patrons between Whitsun and 8th July 1911 were charged an extra 6*d.* for the new tip-up seats. In 1912 came a stage curtain, with 'a centre curtain across the narrowest part of the Stage and two side curtains' the following year. Hanging baskets of ferns were already being replaced by June 1911, and ferns continued to be kept for a number of years until in 1928 hanging baskets of artificial flowers were bought. There are various references to local residents taking in the Pavilion shrubs for the winter

A 1904 photo showing the canvas roof on bandstand area.
(Cromer Museum)

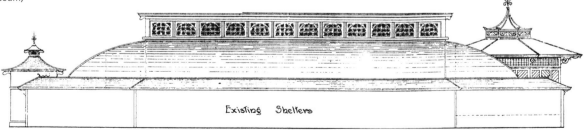

Existing Shelters

The side elevation of the new pavilion roof.

55

The capital of one of the columns for the pier pavilion, from the original designs.

months, and to their gardeners being allowed gratuities of ten shillings for looking after them.

Entertainments Committee and Works Committee minutes; plans and elevations by Douglass & Arnott.

1921

'At the Pier-head there is an excellent Pavilion, with seating accommodation for about a thousand people. This building is lighted by electricity.'

Cromer and Sheringham (Burrows Guides series), 1921. In this year, further improvements were made to the stage and two additional dressing-rooms provided. The electric lighting, installed in 1905, consisted of about a hundred lamps; in 1913 it had been agreed that these be 'frosted and fitted with holophane shades and the small side lamps dispensed with'.

1924

'The Committee inspected the Pier Pavilion Stage and considered the advisability of carrying out enlargements and improvements thereto with a view to adapting it to theatrical performances. After discussion it was decided that further particulars of the required alterations and of the probable cost, also particulars and cost of the installation of a Cinematograph Apparatus be obtained.'

Works Committee minutes, 18th November 1924. This tells us less about what was actually done than about what was thought worth considering at the time!

1949

As part of the post-war reconstruction and improvements, Boulton & Paul of Norwich produced plans for steelwork for a proposed extension at the stage end of the Pavilion.

Boulton & Paul blueprint.

1953-55

Inspection of the damage to the Pavilion after the floods of January 1953 revealed that 'a very large area of roof has virtually no support' and that 'the waves got under the stage and took away its support.'

Letter of 2nd March 1953 to R. Brandon Esq., in Boardman's file. Bullen's estimate for repairing the pavilion, reconstructing the stage, and building a new bar and shelters, was accepted in July 1954.

'The restored Pier Pavilion at Cromer, which comes into use on Wednesday, was open to the public for three hours on Saturday. Both pier and pavilion were severely damaged in the 1953 gales and their restoration has cost more than £50,000. . . .

'The western side of the building, which sustained the full force of the gales, has had to be completely reconstructed and now includes a bar.

'The floor of the pavilion has been entirely relaid and the interior is in cream and grey.

'The hall seats about 800 people in new tip-up seats.'

Eastern Daily Press, 13th June 1955. Final accounts were not submitted to the Cromer Urban District Council until November 1955. After Richard Condon's death on 14th October 1991, the Council dedicated the bar - not the original one of 1955 - at the Pavilion Theatre to his name.

1969

'The Council has invited tenders for alterations which include the erection of a screen across the back of the auditorium - at about row S - which would reduce the seating to about 500-550 and provide facilities for catering behind it.

'The screen would be soundproof and fireproof and, as an added fire precaution, two additional exits direct on to the Pier deck would have to be made from the body of the hall.

'From the minutes of 1914, an example of male chauvinism at its worst: it was resolved unanimously that the Commissioners do not consider the provision of sanitary conveniences for women on the pier, in addition to the existing urinal for men, necessary, taking into consideration the close proximity of the Council's public conveniences.'

Woodhouse notes. The Commissioners had also voted against women's conveniences in 1908. Not until 26th June 1925 was it 'Resolved to recommend that complete conveniences for both sexes be provided on the Pier and on the Parade.'

'"We want to get a more intimate atmosphere in there," explained the chairman of the committee, Mr. Mike Platten, who added that at the moment even 300 people could look a bit sparse.'

Eastern Daily Press, 10th October 1969.

1978

'Dick Condon . . . reckoned that the 70-year-old Pavilion which last season looked as bleak as the east coast on a winter's day, could be transformed into a positive attraction for £30,000 and that is the figure the council has spent on it. . . . I am told the auditorium was formerly pale and dreary. Now, it is a smart and comforting crimson with new seating and new wall-to-wall carpeting. The Pavilion has 437 seats and the last six rows, once on the same level as the rest, are now raked.

'There are new bars at the front (coffee and licensed) and new lavatories; the stage has been extended, its equipment improved and its lighting refurbished.'

Eastern Daily Press, 27th May 1978.

The Council's Leisure Activities Committee was told in November 1978 that top priority in capital spending should be given to two new ladies' toilets in the pier pavilion, together with new stage lighting. Also, they were told, 'an improved ventilation scheme should be included . . . as the old system often caused members of the public to get wet.'

North Norfolk News, 1st December 1978, p. 8, col. 7. Further improvements were made to the foyer (including extending the café) in 1987-90 at a cost of over £78,000.

Lifeboat house

'May 2 [1919]. Produced from the Engineers, drawings and speci-fication of the proposed Lifeboat House and Slipway. . . .'

The intention was to erect the lifeboat house at the side of the pier head, but the Cromer Protection Commissioners objected to this plan on the grounds that it `would materially obstruct the view of persons in the shelters'. The RNLI, startled by this new develop-ment (which would add some 18% to the cost and entail difficul-ties with the sewage outfall pipe which ran out to sea underneath the pier), threatened to withhold the promised motor lifeboat from Cromer altogether and station it elsewhere. Privately, how-ever, their Chief Inspector told them it would in fact be very diffi-cult to find another site. The RNLI had to accept the Commissioners' preferred option of siting the development at the very end of the pier, continuing its centre line out to sea.

'Nov. 14th. Reported that the Engineers had been unable to obtain a quotation for the insurance of the barge and motor boat, pro-posed to be used in the construction of the Boathouse and Slipway, on account of the hazardous nature of the risk and the small value involved. . . .

'Feb. 19th [1920]. Approved of the revised designs for the Boathouse and Slipway, which had been revised partly to meet the Commissioners' request that it should harmonise with the Pier Pavilion.

'Feb. 20th. Reported that the works for the reception of a Motor Lifeboat were in hand. . . .

'Nov: 19. Reported that the work at this Station was behind time.

In June last the staging was wrecked, and a new and more substantial one was being built - 185' having been constructed up to the end of September.

'Nov: 18 [1921]. Produced the Engineers' reports showing that considerable damage was done to the new works by a severe gale and heavy seas between 22nd and 24th October.

'After the Contractors had recovered nearly all the foundation timbers, and got them into position again, a further gale on Nov. 1st carried away nearly all the replacement work, and yet again on Nov. 6th the further restoration was demolished by another gale.'

RNLI Précis Book for Cromer, pp.201-206, 474-479. The contractors for building the pier were Charles Brand & Sons; their tender for the work was £14,500, against the RNLI's original estimate of £5,000. The lifeboat house itself is believed to have been a prefabricated unit supplied by Boulton & Paul.

'The cost of the boathouse and slipway will be approximately £30,000. The cause of the high cost is that it has been necessary to construct them right at the end of the pier since, from the shore itself, it would be impossible to launch [the new motor lifeboat] into sufficiently deep water at all states of the tide.'

Cromer and North Norfolk Post , 4th May 1923, p.2, col.2. The boathouse, measuring 60 x 21 feet internally, was built under the supervision of H. Ransome. When the new lifeboat, the H. F. Bailey , arrived from Cowes, it took the crew three hours to house it, though after a test launch they man-aged the task in only one hour. At this date, only 40 of the RNLI's 235 boats were motorised.

There was an opening ceremony on 26th July 1923, the first por-tion of which 'was held in the Pier Pavilion, when a large assem-bly representative of many towns and districts in Norfolk occu-pied the centre of the hall, and many visitors to Cromer were also present'.

Cromer & North Walsham Post , 27th July 1923, p.5, col.1.

The building of the lifeboat house required the skills of 'hard-hat' divers, being helped here by one of the Cromer fishermen.

The new motor lifeboat was dedicated on 2nd August 1923, when 'the Bishop of Norwich gave a brief address, after which as many as the boathouse would hold went thither for the dedication, naming and launch of the new boat, which took the water to the accompaniment of much cheering along the crowded pier and sea front of the town.'

Since the old lifeboat remained based at the Gangway, Cromer now had two lifeboats. On this occasion 'the shore boat did have the pull, for never on display days has she failed to come in to time, like to some demure maiden, whereas, if truth be told, the new comer had the night out with Father Neptune, whose boisterous good humour would not permit of return!'

Norwich Mercury , 4th August 1923.

The first service launch of the new lifeboat, the *H. F. Bailey*, from the pier-end slipway was at 6.40 a.m. on 19th July 1923, when the smack *Hepatica* of Lowestoft was stranded four miles SE by E of the Haisboro light vessel. The weather was fine and the sea smooth, but the lifeboat's propeller was slightly damaged on the slipway.

Crawford Holden, History of Cromer Lifeboats.

The second *H.F. Bailey* lifeboat and her crew. (An H. H. Tansley photograph in the Randall / Salter Magic Lantern Collection)

The new lifeboat house

In November 1996, the lifeboat was moved out of its shed at the end of the pier for demolition work to begin. Cromer was the most exposed site of any lifeboat station in the country, and the 1923 shed was worn out. Plans had been drawn up involving expenditure of £2 million on a replacement shed more than twice the size, including a tipping launching platform, a longer slipway, offices, mechanic's workshop, crew room, toilets and shower, shop and visitor viewing area.

During the reconstruction, the lifeboat was sent away for a refit, being replaced temporarily by a beach-launched boat based in front of the previous lifeboat house at the foot of the Gangway.

North Norfolk News, 19th September 1996, pp.1, 3. The old boathouse was taken to Southwold, to house a maritime museum

The RNLI's model showing the comparison between the 1998 lifeboat house and the 1921 building.

Arcades

1959

'Cromer U.D.C. Pier Committee ran into some opposition over its new proposal to accept the offer of a Sheringham man to place an amusement arcade, with a juke box and Bingo game, on Cromer Pier during the summer. . . . After debate the recommendation was accepted [but one Councillor said that] "We now have on the promenade two of these places, one for which the Council receives a reasonable rent and the other in private ownership." [Another member thought that] they had to do something to attract people to the pier because the number of people who just wanted to walk on the pier or just sit there were not going to be very many.'

Eastern Daily Press, 14th April 1959.

1976

'Two amusement arcades on the deck are privately owned by Mr. E. Monte, of Walsall, who pays a rent of £1040 for the two sites.'

North Norfolk News, 27th February 1976, p.1. Mr Monte was the Sheringham man whose application had caused such debate in 1959.

1982

Tunmore Automatics (who rented the arcades) were planning a £100,000 development, but before long they were given notice to quit, and by 1984 the amusements were being run by the Council.

1990

'An amusement arcade on Cromer pier was devastated yesterday as hurricane-force winds uprooted the building and flung it 300 yards along the beach.

'The roof and walls of the wooden arcade were ripped from the pier shortly after 9am as 100mph gusts lashed the North Norfolk coastline.

'Three men working on the pier minutes before the arcade blew away probably owe their lives to a quick-thinking council official who told them to leave.

'The pier . . . was immediately sealed off as a sandstorm blew up, showering the promenade with debris and splinters of glass. . . .

'A clean-up operation was halted for a time during the morning amid fears that council workmen, who had to cling to pier railings to protect themselves from the gusting wind, might be swept over the side.'

Eastern Daily Press, 27th February 1990. The council agreed on 7th March not to replace the arcades.

The pier arcade blown down in 1990. (North Norfolk News, Nick Lyons)

Shelters

1901

'Excellent seating and shelter space is provided on the Pier. There are small shelters on both sides, and a very large one at the head. This, which is circular in shape, includes a fine band-stand, and is so constructed as to be covered with an awning if desired.'

Eastern Daily Press, 8th June 1901, p.5, col.8. In fact the pier-head shelter was not so much circular as an irregular octagon. The awning is just visible in the picture on page 55.

1920s

'By the 1920s the two shelters on the decking had been rearranged to run down the centre (where they had previously been situated in the bays).'

Warren, unpublished notes, 1990.

The original bandstand and shelters which formed the pier-head enclosure which was gradually developed into the Pavilion Theatre. Compare the side elevation on page 55.

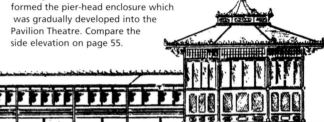

'At the head of the Pier shelters were arranged in such a way that, no matter which way the wind blew, it was possible to get out of it, and at the same time to enjoy the sunshine and obtain the benefit of the air for which Cromer was celebrated.'

Eastern Daily Press, 10th June 1901, p.6, col.6. Electric lighting was provided for the shelters round the pier head in 1911. The original shelters can still be seen: they form the walls of the present Pavilion Theatre foyer.

1914

'The Question of the provision of a Canvas Wind Screen for the Pier in place of the Wood & Glass Screen previously suggested, was considered, and . . . It was Resolved to recommend that a Screen 102 yards in length be obtained.'

Works Committee minutes, 6th May 1914.

1935

'The question of the extension of the Shelters to form a weather screen down the centre of the Pier was considered. It was resolved to recommend that a length of 16 yards be erected at the Pavilion end of the centre Shelters, of similar design and attached to the existing Shelters but without roof or seats.'

Works Committee minutes, 18th March 1935. The bill for the work was passed for payment on 4th September.

1951

'Prefabricated windbreaks are to be erected down the centre of the pier in due course and these will be fixed in a way which will facilitate their removal if the plan of providing a restaurant is carried out.'

Eastern Daily Press, 13th January 1951. New shelters had to be erected after the storm of January 1953 (cf. picturespages 47 and 51).

1995

New shelters were erected in the middle of the pier in May.

Proposed restaurants

In October 1948, Boardman's of Norwich designed a building which would extend down the pier, from near the Pavilion entrance almost to the wider section in the middle of the pier, and would contain a restaurant, bar, kitchen and toilets. The plan also included siting a shop at the entrance, between the turnstiles. The plan was revised in December to put the restaurant on the wider part in the middle of the pier; it would have had 96 seats. It was never built, however.

Boardman's plans and elevations of 1948.

'A proposal was accepted in 1987 for an extension to the catering facilities at the Pavilion. The proposals involved the construction of a café area to the front of the existing structure. A new cafeteria would cater for 55 seats while the area taken up by the existing cafeteria would be utilized by the bar. . . . Work was started on the scheme and . . . the decking was strengthened. . . The scheme,

however, was not completed for financial reasons.'

North Norfolk District Council. Report . . . 6th May 1992 , pp.4-5.

Illuminations

'SIR, - When the Cromer Protection Commissioners are next applied to for leave to allow bands to play on the Jetty and Esplanade it is to be hoped they will insist upon the removal of the paltry lanterns suspended round the Pier. If it is necessary to have music after dark, surely some better means of illumination is available than these wretched reminders of suburban London tea gardens.'

The Argus, Norwich, 29th August 1891.

1901

'A central row of three-light lamps are most effective by day and shed a brilliant illumination at night.'

Eastern Daily Press, 8th June 1901, p.5, col.8. In 1907 the lamp columns were painted dark green instead of the original white.

1909

'In December 1909 the Works Committee was instructed to arrange for the pier to be completely lighted by electricity at a cost not to exceed £42. An amendment for a tender be obtained from the Gas Company was lost. It was also arranged for a flashlight sign with the word "Concert" to be fixed above the entrance to the Pavilion. (This was still in use in 1939.)'

Woodhouse notes. Only the pier head lamp remained lit by gas (there is a reference to it in 1920). A further decision was taken in May 1914 to illuminate the pier with 142 five-candle-power lamps, and two festoons of 25 lights each were to be fitted after Easter in 1921.

1926

'The pier presented a gorgeous sight [during the fete of August 1926], when all the lights, which numbered 650, including those inside the pavilion, were lit, all the fairy lamps were coloured, green, red, blue, yellow, and there was a wonderful variety of Chinese lanterns, a mass of lighting and colouring which was very effective after sunset. The all-important task of carrying out the lighting scheme was in the hands of Mr. W. J. Scarff, the manager of the Cromer Electricity Supply, who must be congratulated on his skill and taste. . . .

'There were coloured lamps in the alcoves, and the large lamps in the building were enclosed in the square mauve frames with orange panels surmounted with designs of birds as they were on the last occasion [*sc.* the 1925 carnival] when their attractiveness induced the Commissioners to have them permanently.'

'Cromer's great carnival,' in Cromer & North Norfolk Post, 27th August 1926.

A photograph from the 1930s, showing the pier illuminated. (Crawford Holden Collection)

ACTIVITIES ON THE PIER

'By some Cromer may be considered dull, as there are few amusements excepting such social ones as strangers can provide for themselves; and those habituated to constant excitement may perhaps here feel the ennui of seclusion. But . . . the libraries, the promenades by the sea-side, the ride or walk to some beautiful vicinage, the sail on the sea, or the telescopic survey of some vast expanse, may surely compensate for the heated atmosphere of the crowded theatre, and for the giddy whirl kept up till daybreak in the close and heated ball-room.'

Blanchard, Adams's descriptive guide, p.178.

'The Commissioners have wisely decided to introduce nothing on the pier which will in any way tend to lower the tone of the place. . . . Those who expect fourth rate theatrical performances on the pier will meet with disappointment; for the Commissioners have resolved to . . . merely provide a band which shall satisfy the most exacting taste. . . . The Commissioners have decided that no advertisements shall be allowed to mar the elegance of the pier, nor are automatic machines to be permitted.'

Norfolk Daily Standard, 8th June 1901. Resistance to automatic machines continued for many years; in the 1920s, it was even resolved not to allow the introduction of a cigarette machine!

A place to travel from

'The jetty, of wood, about 70 yards long, erected in 1822, forms an attractive promenade. . . . Vessels of from 60 to 100 tons burden discharge their cargoes of coal and timber on the beach.'

Bayne, Royal Illustrated History of Eastern England, vol.i, p.211. Evidently the 1822 jetty was regarded as a pleasure facility, and not as a working goods facility.

'There is an annual fair every Whit Monday, to which the novelty of the arrival of pleasure-seekers in handsomely-trimmed boats lends a singular charm.'

Blanchard, Adams's Descriptive Guide, p.176. It is not clear whether they landed at the jetty or on the beach, however.

'The Great Yarmouth "Star" Steam Tug Company (Limited), beg to announce that their powerful and commodious Steamers, "United Service," or "Meteor," . . . will leave the South Quay, near the Crane, at 9.30 a.m., calling at the Britannia Pier at 10 a.m., during the ensuing season, for Cromer, Mondays, Wednesday and Fridays. . . . The Steamer for Cromer will call off Hasborough when required, either to land or embark passengers. . . . Fares there and back Yarmouth and Cromer 2s. 6d. . . . Refreshments may be obtained on board.'

Advertisement in Yarmouth Gazette , 22nd July 1876, p.4, col.2. By 1890 the service was operating daily except Saturdays. The ships probably did not use the pier, however - see the next extract.

'In *Rambles in East Anglia* by Harry Brittain, 1897, he writes of a steamer trip from Yarmouth to Cromer aboard the ill-fated *Victoria*. His voyage was earlier in the same season of 1888 that the *Victoria* struck the Church Rock on the 9th August as she was setting out on her return journey to Yarmouth. . . .
'Brittain's voyage was without such unwanted excitement and on arrival the passengers were conveyed to the shore by a number of small boats, suggesting perhaps that the jetty was insufficient to meet the needs of such as the *Victoria*.'

Rouse, Coastal Resorts of East Anglia, pp.104-105.

In the years 1907-10 there was much discussion of erecting a landing stage so that small boats could tie up. At first it was thought it might be possible to have a small stage alongside the pier, with a ladder for access to the pier above. In 1907 Alfred Thorne, the contractor, gave the Commissioners an estimate for £710. 15s. - far more than they had envisaged. In October they agreed that 'the probable income to be derived from such expenditure [now estimated at £872] does not justify them in carrying out that part of the Scheme.'

By 1st June 1910, the District Council had 'Resolved that in the opinion of this Council it is essential to the welfare of Cromer that adequate landing facilities should be made for small boats at an early date,' so the Commissioners decided to ask W. T. Douglass 'what sort of Landing Stage he would recommend for small boats to be constructed independently of the Pier.' He again came up with something much too elaborate:

'The position which I recommend is one starting from the Bath Hotel bastion & extending seaward to the line of the Pier Heads, practically to the line of the existing Bath Hotel Groyne. . . .

'The total length of the stage which I recommend will be about 690 ft. with a deck width of 6 ft. The seaward end would be situated at a point about 410 ft. to the eastwards of the pier head.'

Even though he was prepared to countenance a landing stage of only half the length, it was still a more expensive proposition than the Commissioners had had in mind. They were informed that their idea of something simple attached to the pier would probably endanger the pier structure, and could well be outside the powers they had been given in the Act of Parliament anyway. The idea was again dropped.

Letter of 13th June 1910 from W. T. Douglass to the Cromer Protection Commissioners, with related notes and newspaper cuttings in Norfolk Record Office; Works Committee minutes.

'Winston Churchill became First Lord of the Admiralty in 1911: his next visit to Cromer was in 1913, when accompanied by his wife, he arrived off Cromer in the "Enchantress" - the Admiralty yacht. . . . Mrs Winston complained to me of the absence of landing facilities at Cromer. . . . She was much amused when I informed her it was entirely her husband's fault, because I well knew as one of the Protection Commissioners, that application had been made to the Admiralty months previously for Government monetary support for a landing stage, on the plea that Naval units were constantly calling at Cromer, and that safe methods of landing would be most desirable. I told her that the Admiralty acknowledged our letter expressing regret that they were unable to promise any assistance.'

H. C. Dent, Reminiscences of a Cromer Doctor, pp.22-23.

In 1919, when the Protection Commissioners' agreement was sought to build the new lifeboat house at the end of the pier, they demanded 'that gangways be provided on both sides of the house for public use, so that the slipway may be used for landing purposes with access to the pier-head.' The RNLI could not sanction the use of their charitable funds for purposes unconnected with the lifeboat, but a compromise was reached. A small gangway would be built at one side of the boathouse, and without the RNLI being responsible for the cost. On 18th November 1921 it was 'reported that money for the gangway had been collected locally and that the Engineers had been instructed accordingly.'

RNLI Précis Book, pp.202-204, 478-479.

Passengers have occasionally disembarked at the pier in much more recent years - though not always without mishap, as the following report from 1955 shows:

'*H.M.S. Pincher's* pinnace was holed in the port side on Friday when a swell lifted her as she was being brought alongside the steps of Cromer Pier. Mr. H. T. Davies, coxswain of the Cromer lifeboat, brought the ship's liberty men ashore in a crab boat.'

North Norfolk News, 29th July 1955, p.1, cols.2-3.

'The question of granting permission for the operation of Speed-Boats from the Pier . . . was discussed. . . . Resolved to recommend that the matter be not entertained for the ensuing Season.'

Works Committee minutes, 27th December 1928. Much too racy an idea for Cromer!

A place to see from

Cromer 'presented an unusually animated scene on Wednesday last, occasioned by the influx of gay company to witness the exercising of the Cromer and Mundesley life-boats,' with trials of Manby's mortar and Hase's improved version. Cromer won the rowing match between the two lifeboat crews, and there were fireworks from the jetty.

Norwich Mercury, 10th September 1823. We can easily imagine the spectators thronging the jetty as well as the shore, though the newspaper report merely says that the jetty was the stage for the firework display.

'The jetty . . . is a fashionable resort in the evening, the company assembling here, some to enjoy the pure sea breezes, to watch the noble billows as they dash in graceful fury on the beach, the fine spectacle of the setting sun, or the splendour of the moon; others to meet their acquaintances.'

Sargant, Guide to Cromer, 1841, p.9.

Special events

'Sunday, Oct 5. Well now I must tell you that there has for some days past been a wreck on the shore . . . & today they got a tug from Yarmouth & took it to be mended. . . . Enormous quantities of people were on the jetty and shore watching the wreck going away.'

Buxton, Journal 1860-1864 , p.62. The consequence of this excitement was that the congregation at church was noticeably thinner than usual!

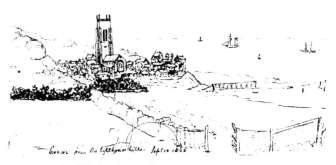

An 1862 drawing by Ellen Buxton, from page 15 of her journal.

In June 1913 it was agreed to accept the offer of the *Daily Mail* to bring their Waterplane to Cromer for a visit, 'to give exhibitions and carry passengers in front of the Pier'.

Entertainments Committee minutes. A newspaper photograph shows the Blackburn Iris flying boat being watched from the pier by Sir Samuel Hoare and others on 29th September 1926.

On the pier, watching the Cromer regatta in 1910. (Crawford Holden Collection)

Carnivals

'Wednesday [26th August 1925] was a notable day in the history of Cromer, for the first illuminated fete on a large scale ever held on the Pier was a success which exceeded the hopes of the most optimistic promoters of the events. . . .
'Fortunately the weather was fine, so everyone was attracted to the fun. The pier presented a gorgeous sight, when all the lights, numbering nearly five hundred, were lit. . . . Mr. A. Hardy, whose genius for decorative work is widely known, had made the Pier gay with bunting, flags and festoons. He was especially successful in transforming the interior of the Pier Pavilion, which usually gives a somewhat cold impression, by a tasteful colour scheme carried out in blue and gold, with gay festoons. The pillars were hidden by curtains of Chinese design. There were ruby coloured lamps in the alcoves, and the large lamps around the sides of the building were enclosed in square mauve frames, with orange panels surmounted with designs of birds. The top frieze consisted of a border containing the arms of Norfolk and Cromer. Over the proscenium was a grey blue sky cloth, with a shining moon and trees, and the stage had screens with blue panels in keeping with the other decorations.'

'King Carnival at Cromer,' in Cromer and North Norfolk Post , 28th August 1925. This was the first of a series of fetes which produced handsome profits. Commander Locker-Lampson, of Newhaven Court, was a key figure in their organisation, and many of his extraordinarily wide circle of friends in high society were induced to come and help - the first carnival was opened by Princess Ileana of Roumania, who had also joined the party going round the district in fancy dress during the previous few days selling tickets for the event. After the first three years the fetes were held in the grounds of Cromer Hall instead of on the pier.

'The presence of the King and Queen of Greece on this occasion was without doubt the main factor in creating such widespread interest in Cromer's second carnival since the war. . . .

'As a compliment to the Royal visitors a special archway was constructed at the entrance to the dance arena in the pavilion, this consisting of mauve columns and art blue draperies with a Crown on either side.

'At least six thousand people had assembled on the pier and promenade when the proceedings commenced. . . .

'Two maroons were fired as the King and Queen of Greece were driven in a motor car down the west end slope on to the promenade. . . .

'Their Majesties, preceded by the guard of honour, made their way through the densely packed pier to the pavilion. There was no doubt as to the enthusiasm of their welcome. Cheers rang out, men raised their hats or saluted, and the King and Queen with characteristic graciousness smiled with pleasure at their warm reception. . . .

'The fancy dress parade was held. . . .

'Over a thousand people then enjoyed watching exhibition dancing. . . .

'Major H. C. Dent announced that the number of people admitted to the pier between 7 and 9 p.m. was 4,402. . . .

'Dancing then continued until past midnight.'

'Cromer's great carnival,' in Cromer and North Norfolk Post , 27th August 1926.

'Everyone wanted to see the Devil's Dive, performed by Mr. William A. Kenna, a swimming instructor, well known to visitors, and the pier was literally packed from end to end when the time came for this feat to be performed. A stage had been erected almost level with the top of the pavilion. The Princess Marina Chavchavadje [of Russia, who had opened the fête] and a few privileged persons mounted to the roof of the pavilion in order to see this spectacle. The sea looked dark and very cold and uninviting and the drop seemed a long way. Ugh! The crowds watched with breathless expectation while the Devil, all in red, enveloped him with a blazing cloak, and then plunged boldly down, down into the water, and vociferous applause and cheers were given for the diver. . . .

'Commander Locker-Lampson had offered a prize of £5 to the person giving the correct or nearest estimate of the number of persons passing on to the pier between 6 and 8.30 p.m. The official figures were 4,631, and three people had estimated 4,630. . . . They were awarded £2 each.'

'Cromer's great carnival,' in Cromer and North Norfolk Post , 26th August 1927. There was also a carnival and fete on 24th August 1932, when in addition to the entertainments in the Pavilion there were displays on the pier deck by wire-walkers and an escapologist called Radini.

Through the 1980s and 1990s the Red Arrows aerial display team has been a regular at Cromer Carnival. The pier has always formed an excellent viewing platform, or a backdrop for photographing the aircraft. Here one of the team swoops low over the building of the new lifeboat house. The jib of the crane had been specially lowered for the display!

Sketching the view

'We all had a walk on the Jetty early and not without Company - I sketch'd the easternmost part of the Coast & while my Ladies were preparing for walking did the same from the Pier of the western Cliffs.'

Mr Marten's Journal , 16th September 1825.

Sketches of Cromer from the pier, from the Marten diary.

In a diary of 1839, a gentleman from Norwich refers to his holidays in Cromer where, in between walking on the cliffs and beach with his sisters, and visiting the Bath House for a warm bath or to read the papers or chat with the proprietor, he would sketch from the pier using his 'camera', i.e. a portable device which reflected the view onto a piece of paper to make it easy to draw. Thus one Saturday produces the diary entry: 'Rose about 5: on jetty with camera.'

Diary of James Stone, quoted by Brian Hall in North Norfolk News, 29th August 1952, p.4, cols.4-5.

A place to be seen and a place to meet

'A fine Morning - inducing to a walk on the Jetty before Breakfast. There were several Ladies walking, & if not in full dress yet in dresses evincing care, & custom to appear well dressed.'

Mr Marten's Journal , 17th September 1825.

'There is also an excellent Jetty, built exclusively for a promenade; there is at all times company walking on this jetty, where you may depend upon meeting all you are acquainted with at some time of the day. . . . The best getting down [i.e., the easiest access to the beach from the cliff top] is opposite to the Jetty for walking . . . a very keen, cold air, very bracing, but fit only for people in good health, and would be comfortless in winters, & in the summer the season is short.'

Anonymous diary, June 1827. The writer was back in Cromer in May 1829, when the first thing he did after putting up at the New Inn was to take a walk on the jetty.

'The mode of life here is rather peculiar. During the early portion of the day, although the place is so well filled, a pleasant silence prevails. About eleven the town appears to open its eyes, and people, chiefly visitors, are seen in the streets. . . . The inhabitants now gradually progress towards full life. The sands become occupied by after breakfast bathers, pedestrians, and donkey riders. The pier itself is solitary, because imperative fashion has declared that the *elite* must not approach that well attended promenade until after the dinner hour of seven; but beneath the pier, upon the bare sandy floor on which stand the piles supporting the structure, and on the cross timbers, collect a heterogeneous community of individuals, fashionable visitors, dawdlers, sketchers, lady workers, nursemaids, and children. . . . As the sun climbs the ladder towards noon . . . the shores are more thickly peopled. . . . Then follows another lull. Ladies and children after awhile seek the shady retreats of their own apartments, and while the youthful seek repose, the former prepare for the "high noon" of the evening, when the pier becomes crowded by the *elite* of the place, and the entire fashionable community promenade (attendez) up the right side and down the left, to the strains of a not very excellent band, until the hour of eight or nine is reached, and then all persons retire from public gaze.'

'Cromer - sketched', 1859. Knights' Illustrated Guide , p.34, notes that the jetty was deserted at low tide, when everybody was on the sand, walking or driving.

'. . . a young lady who pretends to read a book on the seaside pier, though she manages to look up undesignedly at every passer-by . . .'

Scott, Blossom Land and Fallen Leaves, p.6.

A place to talk and to listen

James Stone's diary of his visit to Cromer in 1839 contains an intriguing reference to a woman preaching on or very near the jetty. On Monday 22nd July, he writes: 'Evening superb sunset - woman preaching.' On the following day, he writes: 'Newsroom - evening long talk with Simons on Esplanade - on jetty (woman again).'

Simeon Simons was the proprietor of the Bath House, which also offered a reading room where several daily papers were available. Simons was Cromer's schoolmaster, fizzing with enthusiasm for many subjects, including

the latest thinking on the local geology. It would be interesting to know who the woman was; there are records of Elizabeth Fry preaching at meetings in Cromer near this time, but her journal shows that she was in Grenoble on the day in question.

A place to relax

In a diary entry for Sunday 25th June 1826 we read: 'Edmund Lown [the diarist's brother-in-law?] and his girl came to see my wife and myself. I went home and had some tea and then went down to the jetty for a walk and then we went a part of the way to the Lighthouse and we went too on the sand and then we went on the cliff.'

The Banville Diaries, p.63. Larry Banville was Sir Thomas Buxton's gamekeeper.

'The pier atmosphere is convalescent: old people taking it easy on white benches.'

Andrew Martin, 'Piers of the Realm' in the Sunday Times colour magazine, 25th August 1996, p.3.

. . . but not to smoke!

'A person, who is paid by the Commissioners for the protection of the town, acts as Keeper of the Jetty and Esplanade, whose business it is to prevent improper persons from obtruding themselves, and to preserve good order. We know not whether he has the power to forbid the smoking of cigars, but we certainly think that such ought to be the case; and we would add, that we can hardly believe that any real gentleman would require an admonition on such a point. Servants in livery and all common persons are not allowed at this time. On Sunday the Jetty is, with just consideration, resigned to the inhabitants of the town.'

Sargant, Guide to Cromer, 2nd ed., 1851, p.12. In the original edition of 1841, the jetty keeper had been paid 'gratuituously' (i.e., by tips), but the

Commissioners decided to offer a salary of £10 a year and forbid him to solicit tips. On 13th August 1846 they appointed Richard Cook to the post; after less than a year they had to discharge him for asking visitors for money, and for 'general neglect of duty'.

'The Commissioners very properly forbid smoking on the Jetty, until nine o'clock in the evening, at which time ladies usually retire from their evening promenade.'
Sargant, Guide to Cromer, 5th ed., 1867, p.12. The penalty for smoking was twenty shillings.

To sit and read

A fictional character tells how 'Often during a whole morning we would sit at the end of the little pier (to which the sea comes occasionally) without speaking a word, [my sister] intent on her book or embroidery, I apparently dozing' (though in fact sulking at his predicament, having been rendered blind by an illness in the prime of his youth). 'Several weeks we spent in this fashion.' In later years he comes to 'laugh at the old wooden jetty dignified with the name of pier, most useful as a protection from the sun's rays to the loungers on the sands below.'
Oppenheim, Those Other Days , 1912, pp.15, 17.

Fifty folding canvas chairs were ordered in 1928, with the aim of making a profit on the fees charged for using them.
Entertainments Committee minutes.

As late as 1959, one Councillor thought that 'hundreds of people who stayed in Cromer liked to go on the pier to sit and read. "Soon," he went on, "there will be nowhere in Cromer where a certain type of visitor who wants to sit and read quietly will be able to go, except in North Lodge Park." . . . Mr. Russell Reeve, chairman of the Pier Committee, said it had to be realised it was 1959, not 1919.'
Eastern Daily Press, 14th April 1959.

To fish for pleasure

Annual season tickets were being issued in 1920 at a price of 10/6 including admission to the pier; the price of daily tickets was increased in this autumn from 3*d.* to 4*d.*, and Sunday tickets from 4*d.* to 6*d.* (Sunday tickets had first been issued in 1915; the price then was 3*d.*)
Entertainments Committee minutes. The old jetty had been used by fishermen in a rather different way: Mr Marten in 1825 reported that after lobsters had been caught, they would be kept fresh until wanted by being put in a basket tied to the jetty.

At a meeting of the Protection Commissioners, `Mr. S. Bastow asked whether season fishing tickets would be issued during the coming winter.

`Mr. A. Jarvis said that while the balance sheet might show a certain income from that source yet on the other side there was not shown the cleaning up and necessary re-painting through the fishing business. The fishermen were not at all particular where they put their bait, and while the fishing was going on no one could use the shelters for the purpose for which they were constructed. It was one man's job to look after them. If the actual amount spent on labour was shown there would not be a large balance on the right side. . . . If they got as many fish as they did at Deal they might advertise it for that purpose, but they only got people on there to kill time.'
Cromer and North Norfolk Post, 6th August 1920, p.5, col.4.

A guide of the 1920s states: 'The best angling season is the late autumn, from the middle of October to the end of December. Then the codling approach the shores and fine catches are usually made. . . . Those who wish to come to Cromer for sea-angling during the codling season should send in advance a stamped directed envelope to the Pier Master inquiring if the day chosen is likely to be a good one for sport. Much depends, even when the codling are present off shore, on the state of the tide. . . .

'Angling is not permitted on the Pier during the summer season after 9 a.m.'
A Pictorial and Descriptive Guide to Cromer . . . , p.4.

In 1944-45, 'there was sea fishing from Cromer pier, the "bridge" over the blown-out centre portion being made safe by removal of the "temporary" wooden planks, the RNLI being asked to contribute towards the cost. Not that fishing was proving very rewarding, the second competition organised by the Cromer Sea Angling Club producing a "highest catch" of only 3lbs.'
Brooks, Coastal Towns at War, p.75.

On 7th October, 1951, the pier was the venue for the Jack Hall Cup angling match. The Council had originally refused permission for this, believing the hooks and lines represented a threat to public safety.

'Mr Bateman, secretary of the Cromer Sea Angling Club, which arranged the match, commented this week that he found the Council's attitude hard to understand. On Sunday, he said, there were nearly 50 fishermen, including a number of inexperienced boys, fishing from the Pier. The competition would have involved fewer than 40 experienced anglers.

'The ban aroused considerable indignation among club members and brought to a head the club's grievance over its present terms with the Council for Pier fishing during October, November and December. The club guarantees the Council £60 receipts for this period.'
North Norfolk News, 14th September 1951, p.5, col.3. The trophy was won this year by an American Army sergeant who had joined the club just before the start of the competition.

'On view in a Cromer fishmonger's shop on Friday was a 23 lb. tope which for three days had been straightening anglers' hooks "as if they were made of tin".

'The fish was on the slab because of the determination of Mr A. F. E. Smart, a Northampton visitor . . . It took him about 30 minutes to land, and he had to fight with the fish along the whole length of the pier and land it on the beach.'
North Norfolk News, 31st August 1951, p.6, cols.4-5. The record was broken twice in the 1963 season; on 14th September Bob Taylor of West Street, Cromer, landed a 42-lb. specimen on the pier. By the mid-1970s the council were selling nearly six thousand pier fishing tickets a year.

Fishing from the pier, 1998. (Poppyland Photos)

Keeping order on the jetty

On 10th September 1846 the Protection Commissioners approved the following Bye Laws:

'1. That the Keeper of the Jetty and other works be in attendance there every morning during the months of May, June, July, August, September and October at the hour of Seven; and at the hour of Eight in the morning during the remainder of the year.

'2. That he do every morning throughout the year proceed to remove and complete the removal of all filth and rubbish from the Jetty and the Esplanades by Eight o'Clock, and do keep the same well swept and cleansed throughout the day.

'3. That he do give so many hours attendance every day throughout the year as will be sufficient for the above purposes, and for the due regulation of the Jetty; and do also employ himself in repairing the Esplanades, and the Slopes of the Cliffs, and in cleansing the drains and Sewers on and along the same.

'4. That he be punctual in his attendance every Evening during the months of May, June, July, August, September and October, at the hour of Six in the Evening and continue in attendance so long as any Company remains on the Jetty.

'5. That whilst in attendance at the Jetty he be always respectably dressed, civil and obliging to the Company, and that (being paid for his Services by a Salary) he do not directly or indirectly beg or attempt to obtain from the Company money or any other gift.

'6. As smoking Tobacco on the Jetty before the hour of nine in the Evening during the months of May, June, July, August, and September is prohibited, he do respectfully but firmly represent to all persons infringing this Bye Law, that the practice is not allowed by the Commissioners, and that the penalty will be enforced for disobedience of this Bye Law.

'7. That he use every endeavour to prevent the commission of the several offences against the Act of Parliament specified in the public notice thereof to be affixed in some conspicuous place in the immediate neighbourhood of the Works, and to enforce obedience to the Bye Laws of the Commissioners, by taking proceedings to recover the penalties for the Commission of such offences, and for the Breach of such Bye Laws.'

Commissioners' minutes.

William Breese was appointed Keeper of the Jetty in 1847. In 1856 so many complaints had been received of 'disorderly conduct on the Jetty, and of the frequent absence of the Jetty Keeper from his Post', that the Commissioners had to warn him that if ill-health prevented him from doing his job he should resign; the following April he was dismissed. Nor was the next Jetty Keeper, Robert Pank, any better - he had to be dismissed after nine months.

'Resolved that as Several complaints have been made of the inefficient way in which the Jetty has been lately kept by Thomas Curtis the Jetty Keeper the Clerk be instructed to write to Curtis (who is at present in The Norfolk and Norwich Hospital) telling him that, unless something is done to keep the Jetty in better Order the Commissioners will take the matter into consideration next meeting.'
Commissioners' minutes, 6th October 1869.

'Resolved that the Jetty Keeper, James Curtis, be presented with a Cheque for £2 as a Gift from the Commissioners, to him, for his great attention and endeavouring to keep the Jetty and other places under his Charge respectable during the past year, also that he be re-elected as Jetty Keeper for the ensuing year at the Salary of £10. and a Jetty Keeper to be elected annually.'

Commissioners' minutes, 5th April 1871. Curtis (who was himself to become a Commissioner in later life) remained Jetty Keeper until 1877, when the Commissioners employed Thomas Kennedys at a wage of 1s. 6d. a week to keep the jetty and esplanade clean. A later Keeper, Henry Brackenbury, died in office early in 1887, being succeeded by Henry Balls - still at a salary of just £10. Henry too died in office, in 1889, and was succeeded by Samuel Harrison, who was paid 8 s. a week from June to September and 4 s. a week for the rest of the year.

On 28th June 1893 it was 'Resolved That the attention of the Police authorities be called to the disorder on the Jetty in the evenings especially on Sundays and to request that a policeman attend in that neighbourhood.'

On 11th July the Chief Constable's office in Norwich sent a frosty reply, saying: 'if the Cromer Protection Commissioners employed a proper person to look after their interest on their Jetty at Cromer - that matters would be very different'. The officers in Cromer do what they can; if the Commissioners want to pay for extra service, a special man will be detailed for that duty - '& one who will be able to keep order'!

Commissioners' minutes. By 1912 the Commissioners were employing Pier and Parade Attendants, and Pier Inspector and a Parade Inspector, all in uniform; in 1919 an extra man was engaged as Pier Attendant for the evening performances. During the war, there were the inevitable staff shortages: the Clerk reported to the Works Committee on 1st January 1919 that 'it had not been convenient for the men to take their 2 days annual leave during the past 4 years', and the Commissioners agreed to allow them 'payments at the rates of wages in force during the past four years in lieu thereof'.

W.H. Sweet, Turnstile Attendant. (Cromer Museum)

Fun and games
Roller skating

'In November 1907, roller skating sessions were started during the winter months. Only approved skates were to be used and those using their own skates paid 2*d*. plus 1*d*. admission to the pier; those hiring skates paid 5*d*. Maple flooring was laid down in the pavilion, hatches being provided to act as a safety valve in the event of very high tides.

'In February 1908 a Mr F. W. Barber was refused permission to supply refreshments to roller skaters. (I have always understood, though I have found no mention of it in the minutes, that there was a bye-law forbidding the sale on the pier of anything other than programmes. Certainly during the C.P.C.'s existence, nothing was sold there.)

'Two fancy dress skating carnivals were held each year, and in spite of the lack of refreshments and heating in the pavilion, they seem to have been very popular. (I often heard my parents talk of them and say how good they were.)'

Woodhouse notes. (The skating was during autumn, winter and spring only, because during the summer the pavilion was, of course, being used for stage entertainments.) The pier was even open for roller skating on Christmas and Boxing days, at least in 1919 and 1920.

Rules for the control of roller skating were approved in September 1910, and displayed in the Enclosure. In November 1910 the Entertainments Committee agreed to engage a band of five performers at a fee of 15*s*. to play during skating on Thursday evenings, commencing on 8th December, charging an extra 2*d*. per person. Season tickets for skating were initially priced at 15*s*.,

The pavilion interior ready for skating, with Mr Sweet (Crawford Holden Collection)

but demand must have been fairly small, for the price was reduced in September 1910 to 10/6 and in October 1911 to 6*s*.; in September 1913 they were discontinued altogether. Skating continued into the 1930s, however, with a Skating Club having weekly private sessions.

Entertainments Committee minutes.

'In the years of 1914-18 it was open to all-comers, and the excellent roller skating rink in the pavilion was thronged by people of all ages and of varying degrees of skill. A delicate hint that the same facility would be appreciated again by men of the Forces has been met by the remark that the Commissioners have few, if any, skates that would fit Army boots.'

Eastern Daily Press, ?1947. As late as 1976, when audiences for the theatre were declining, there was a suggestion that roller skating might be reintroduced instead.

Bowling

In 1913 it was agreed that Cromer Bowling Club should be allowed to use the Pier Pavilion every Tuesday and Friday from 2pm to 10pm from October to April. The club terminated their agreement early in 1916.

Entertainments Committee minutes.

Amusement machines

Even in the days of the old wooden jetty there were attempts to introduce amusement machines:

'The Clerk read a letter from the London Automatic Machine Company to the Pier Master at Cromer expressing a desire to place some of their machines on the Pier paying a rental of £5 for each machine.

'The Clerk was instructed to inform the Automatic Company that there was no Pier at Cromer but that the Commissioners who had charge of the Cromer Jetty could not entertain any proposal to place these machines thereon.'

Commissioners' minutes, 6th January 1892. It was true that Cromer had only a simple jetty and not the sort of pleasure pier that some other resorts enjoyed - but an earlier minute on the very same page calls Cromer's structure a 'Pier'. Evidently they were being deliberately stuffy. Similarly, on 8th June the same year they refused an application from the Automatic Photographic Co. Ltd. to place a photographic 'machine' on the pier.

'A new type of visitor was coming to Cromer who expected modern amusement and entertainment. . . . If variety entertainment continued to have competition at the same strength as at present they might have to consider other uses for the Pier Pavilion.'

Eastern Daily Press, 14th April 1959.

The Guinness clock

The Guinness clock (Courtesy Guinness)

Designed originally for the 1951 Festival of Britain, the Guinness Clock featured the zoo animals from Guinness advertisments of the time. It proved so popular that Guinness commisioned several travelling versions, one of which was brought to Cromer pier in the 1950s and helped add about £200 to the pier income.

Entertainments

Alex Jarvis (Randall/Salter Magic Lantern Collection)

An Entertainments Committee was in existence at least by 1910, under the chairmanship of A. E. Jarvis, the manager of the Hotel de Paris, who auditioned and engaged artistes for the special entertainments. He put in a large amount of voluntary work, including auditioning potential artistes in London. He remained chairman until 1923, when he resigned after criticism that he was not allowing the committee a say in the arrangements. Even after this little unpleasantness, he continued to do much hard work for the committee.

The manager of the Town Hall, Vera Florence (soprano), Louis Jones Valentine and Gladys Liles from the West End Revellers. (Woodhouse Collection)

In April 1926 Louis Jones Valentine was appointed General Assistant to the Committee in connection with the Pier Entertainments. He later became Entertainments Manager, being succeeded in 1930 by Claude Howard (who stayed until he had to be made redundant in 1940). Managers after the war included Jack Crosbie, Alfie Howard, Rupert Harvey, Max Casson and local printer Ted Cheverton.

Entertainments Committee minutes; programmes.

1904

'On 22nd July of that year, a decision of some moment was taken. A certain Mrs Brown Potter, who must have been a lady of great renown, was engaged to recite on the pier in the afternoon and evening of 12th August for a fee of 36 guineas - way beyond what the Protection Commissioners were usually prepared to pay. Prices for admission to the enclosure accordingly rocketed from the usual price of 3*d*. to 2/6, 2/- and 1/-, and 6*d*. for the

Promenade round the pier head (these charges not to include the 2*d*. entrance to the pier). The lady must have had a stentorian voice if it was thought possible to hear her outside the enclosure. I only hope there was not a rough sea on that day.'

Woodhouse notes. Cora Urquhart Potter (1857-1936) was an American actress of 'good family' and considerable beauty; she claimed to have raised $50,000 for charity through her amateur performances in the United States, before making her professional debut in London in 1887. Her London agents were Ashtons, and in addition to her acting she was famed for her recitations from such poets as Longfellow, in which she was accompanied by a pianist.

Music

1830

'There is likewise a jetty, which, at high water, forms a delightful promenade, and the scene is occasionally enlivened by a band of music, supported by voluntary contributions.'

Pigot & Co.'s National Commercial Directory, p.8.

1884

'Music is rare, and, I am bound to add, of the worst possible kind.'

Anonymous article in the weekly journal Truth, 4th September 1884 (reprinted in Holiday Notes , 1886, p. 37).

1885

The jetty is 'an unpretending wooden structure, whereon a band occasionally plays. The people will tell you with a touch of pride, that the conductor is the only stranger - he comes from Norwich - and that the rest of the band is composed of residents of the town. Its musical performances are - well, perhaps not first-rate; but as visitors are not hypercritical, they come out to enjoy the evening air and to patrol the jetty in larger numbers, it must be said, on those evenings when the band plays, on the principle probably that "half a loaf is better than none", and that such a break in the general quiet of one's existence at Cromer is to be welcomed.'

Article in the magazine All the Year Round , 15th August 1885, reprinted in Holiday Notes , 1886, pp. 43-44.

1890

On 25th June, 'an application from Mr J Pidgeon and others to be allowed to give short concerts at the foot of the Jetty was not acceded to.'

On 2nd July, 'an application by Mr. Charles Greenhead for permission to give two concerts daily on the Jetty was not acceded to.

'It was resolved to give permission to the Band of the I Company 3rd. V.B.N.R. to play on the Jetty approaches on Saturdays and on such one other day (not Thursdays) in the week as the Band may select. And also to give permission to the Anchor Brewery Norwich to play on the Jetty approach on Thursdays.'

Commissioners' minutes. In the event, it turned out that there had been a misunderstanding: the Anchor Brewery Band was committed in Norwich on Thursdays, but the Commissioners hoped they would be able to find another day when they could play. Clearly not every aspirant band was allowed to play - standards had to be upheld!

1891

'No one ventured to depart from the monotony of the orthodox seaside programme. They had done their sand, done their cliffs, called for their letters, read their newspaper, eaten their accustomed meals; and now there was nothing to be accomplished except to walk on a wooden pier and to listen to the music of an active but not very distinguished band.'

Scott, Blossom Land and Fallen Leaves, p.32. Scott favoured the unspoilt countryside of undeveloped Overstrand and Sidestrand rather than the conventional pleasures of Cromer.

1901

When the new pier was opened, 'half an hour was spent on the Pier listening to the excellent playing of the Blue Viennese Band, under Herr Moritz Wurm. . . . [Mr Jarvis promised that] inside the inclosure there would be no fourth or fifth rate theatrical performances, but a really good band.'

Eastern Daily Press, 10th June 1901, p.6, cols.4-6. The band was booked through the Keith Prowse agency at £56 a week, this sum not varying for the four years it came. In February 1904 the Commissioners decided that a vocalist should be engaged for all evening performances of the band; remuneration would be 17¹/₂% of receipts taken in the enclosure.

When Miss Margaret Cooper appeared on the pier in August 1908, 'It was resolved that the pier be decorated and illuminated, and the Cromer Electrical Supply agreed to provide 100 lamps and labour in fixing at the price of £5. The Chairman was also authorised to purchase hanging baskets of ferns for the decoration of the interior of the pavilion at a total not exceeding £4.'

Woodhouse notes. Margaret Cooper had developed a personal style of humorous 'songs at the piano', taking spontaneous liberties with both words and music as she played and sang. Cromer were lucky to get her in August, for she looked forward to 31st July as the end of her working year: 'As soon as August is in, I am at my beloved Broadstairs,' she wrote in her autobiography.

1910

'The amusements are not great, the best thing being the Italian Band on the pier.'

Postcard sent in 1910; quoted in Rouse, Coastal Resorts of East Anglia, p.85. Ashton's Royal Italian Band, conducted by Signor Calamari, played twice daily in 1911. In 1914 there were troupes from Ashton's for the first three weeks of the season, then a band of eight players plus a vocalist for the remainder of Ashton's period; then for nine weeks the Protection Commissioners themselves engaged a band of at least 13, with two or three artistes. The hiring of the band ceased during the First World War, but military concerts were put on instead.

The Italian band, resident at the pier bandstand (Crawford Holden Collection)

Ashton & Mitchell Ltd were the agents most commonly used to provide artistes and resident bands from 1905 up till World War 2. In July 1911 it was agreed that the agents should take 30% of ticket sales and pay the artistes out of this share. Signor Calamari's band was the staple for several years, and the Sheringham Prize Band played many times between the wars.

Entertainments Committee minutes. The conductor was known locally as 'Signor Calamity'!

The pier has proved a romantic matchmaker on at least one occasion. Amleto Fabbri, an Italian cellist, was playing with the Royal Italian Band on the pier in 1908. He went into a Garden Street tea shop - Kingston House, on the corner of the High Street - and there met Mabel Nockels, daughter of a Cromer fishmonger. Fabbri was back on the pier in 1909, and must have resumed his acquaintance with Mabel, for in the following year they married and moved to Italy. The eldest of their ten grandchildren writes: 'They deeply loved each other and were regarded as a perfect couple and they are now buried together in Ravenna cemetery.'

Information in Cromer Museum from Paolo Fabbri of Bologna

CROMER PIER.

SEASON, 1911.

ASHTON'S CELEBRATED
Royal Italian Band,

(CONDUCTOR: SIGNOR GAETANO CALAMANI)

PERFORMS DAILY DURING THE SEASON.

WEEK DAYS: Afternoons, 3 to 4.30. Evenings, 7.45 to 10.15.
Also on Saturday Mornings, 11.30 to 1.
SUNDAYS: Evening, 8 to 10.

First-Class Vocalist every Evening.

In addition to the Royal Italian Band and Weekly Vocalists, the following well-known Special Entertainers have been engaged :—

Mr. FRED CHESTER (Humorous Entertainer)
Six Days Commencing JULY 10.
SPECIAL ATTRACTION,
Six Days Commencing JULY 17.
Mr. ASTLEY WEAVER (Musical Entertainer)
Six Days Commencing JULY 24.
Mr. COOPER MITCHELL (Society Entertainer)
Six Days Commencing JULY 31.
Mr. ERNEST HASTINGS (Musical Humorist)
Six Days Commencing AUGUST 7.
Mr. REX KING (" The One Man Programme ")
Six Days Commencing AUGUST 14.
Miss GERTRUDE TOMALIN (Reciter & Entertainer)
Seven Days Commencing AUGUST 21.
Mr. ARCHIE NAISH (Musical Entertainer)
Six Days Commencing AUGUST 28.
Mr FODEN WILLIAMS (The North of England
Entertainer)
Six Days Commencing SEPTEMBER 4.
Miss VIOLET CARMEN (Society Entertainer,
Reciter, etc.)
Six Days Commencing SEPTEMBER 11.
Matinees THURSDAY and SATURDAY AFTERNOONS.

ROLLER SKATING.

SPECIAL FLOORING IN PAVILION. - - SKATES ON HIRE.

Advertisement for band concerts in 1911 Cromer official guide.

1918

'The Pier Pavilion was crowded on Sunday evening with an audience who testified in no half-hearted fashion its warm appreciation of the excellence of the concert presented. The vocal contributions of Miss Grace Utting and Miss Mary Goulden were most deservedly much admired; the violin solos of Sergt. H. Norris (late leader of D'Oyley Carte Orchestra) were a delight. . . .

'The Pierrots and Orchestra of the Red Horse Shoe Division commenced on Wednesday night four nights' engagement in the Pier Pavilion. They have come direct from the Western front, and the programme they present is that which they have given to the men in the fighting zone in France. It was received on Wednesday night by a crowded audience with every demonstration of approval and delight. Certainly nothing of such an attractive character has been seen on the Pier since pre-war times. The troupe has a total strength of sixty.' The programme included songs, cello solos, and dances.

Unidentified photocopy in Cromer Museum of a newspaper report dated Friday 16th August 1918. The Band of the West Somerset Yeomanry had played on three occasions in 1917.

'The playing of the band of the Liverpool Regiment gave much pleasure. These concerts on the pier serve a double purpose, in giving the public a welcome war-time diversion, and at the same time bringing in much-needed revenue to the public funds.'

Cromer, Sheringham and District Weekly Press, 16th February 1918, p.1, col.5. On 7th September this year, the same newspaper reported that August pier receipts represented almost a three-halfpenny rate.

1921

'A Band plays there daily, and three times on Saturday, when a special afternoon concert is given.'

'Concerts are given from 7.45 to 10.15p.m. on weekdays and Band performances from 3 to 4.30. On Sunday evenings sacred concerts are given from 8 to 10.'

Cromer and Sheringham (Burrows Guides series), 1921. Other guides show that 'the pier orchestra will play daily' in 1928 and 'Mornings and Afternoons' in 1930. The highest-priced seats at the concerts had gone up from 1s. (plus admission to the pier) in 1913 to 2s. (including admission to the pier and entertainments tax) in 1919; from 1921 to 1923 there were even 3s. charges during August.

1928

The Cromer Amateur Operatic and Dramatic Society booked the Pier Pavilion in 1928 - for an instrumental concert on the Sunday after Easter.

Entertainments Committee minutes. Since that time, music has been almost entirely confined to single concerts by visiting performers, mostly on Sunday evenings.

Cinema

'It seems curiously mean that [the Protection Commissioners] refused to accede to Ashton & Co.'s request that admission be raised from 3d. to 4d. on the occasion of a cinematograph display although they were willing for the display to be given.'

Woodhouse notes. An early photograph of the pier shows a large notice at the gates advertising this CINEMATOGRAPH.

'The Clerk had a letter from the Cromer Electricity Supply that they could not supply current direct from their mains for Cinematographic Entertainments and suggesting that the Operators should bring a Motor Generator with them.'

Works Committee minutes, 3rd July 1912.

Theatre
Early theatrical performances in Cromer

A touring company - Scraggs' Original Norfolk and Suffolk Company, which had just separated from David Fisher's Norfolk and Suffolk Company of Comedians and had been playing a July season in Holt - put on a varied bill of plays during August 1812 at a theatre in Cromer, but there is no indication of where this theatre was.

Newspaper advertisement reproduced in Goodwyn, Cromer Past .

A newspaper report of 7th September 1816 describes Cromer Theatre as 'fashionably attended' and says that 'the house, or rather, barn, which is neatly fitted up, is under the management of Mr Eldred.'

Mackie, Norfolk Annals. John Eldred, who was a surveyor of the highways in 1812, died on 31st December 1828, aged 80, and is buried in the churchyard.

A handbill of 1822 advertises a theatrical performance taking place at the **Wellington Inn**, Garden Street. Prices are given as 1s. for the Pit and 6d. for the Gallery. The play is A Cure for the Heart ache, a comedy which had also been in the repertory of the Fisher theatre company at the turn of the century. Members of the company performing in Cromer include Mr Dounton, Mrs Young, Mr Laverock, Mrs Dillon and Mrs Double, and 'the Gentlemen of the Band have kindly consented to attend'.

Playbill in Cromer Museum. The prices are the same as for the second half of the double or triple bills at purpose-built theatres such as the one at North Walsham. The Norwich Mercury of 22nd March 1817 had advertised the bankruptcy sale of the Wellington; by 1826 it was in the hands of Robert Sunman.

`The chief excitement in the way of entertainment [up until 1889] was the occasional visit of a company of "barn-stormers", who thought nothing of rendering several Shakespearean tragedies during a three-day visit. These performances were given in a barn-like structure opposite the position now occupied by the East Coast Garage Co.'

Dent, Reminiscences, ch.1. There were three or four barns in the vicinity of what is now Mount Street.

A newspaper report of 1890 says that 'Mr James Skea and his dramatic company are now performing a series of popular plays at the Assembly-room,' which presumably means the Assembly Room at the **Red Lion**.

Norfolk Daily Standard , 29th January 1890.

From 1901, Charles Thurston, a Norwich showman, travelled around the area with his 'Original Royal Show', which included a cinematograph, and Cromer was one of the places where he stayed for the winter. Ernest Priest was another cinema showman whose itinerary included Cromer.

Live shows, boxing and films were exhibited at the **Cromer Theatre of Varieties**, opened in 1914 in Hans Place. (It later became the Regal cinema.) Talkies were installed in 1930 - the first time they had come to the area.

Peart, The Picture House in East Anglia, pp.14, 24, 86.

In 1893 Lottie Collins starred in a pantomime, *Blue Beard*, at the Town Hall theatre, where Lillie Langtry played for just one week in 1906. In 1928 this venue was advertising productions from 2nd July until September. The lessees and managers at that time were Baring Brothers. During the 1930s there were cinema shows in the Town Hall during the summer season. Plays continued to be staged at the Town Hall until it was sold to Rust's in 1963.

The '**Olympian Pavilion**' in Garden Street had once been the garden of the Rust family, who erected a stage to turn it into an open-air venue for concerts: a professional concert party was engaged for the 1906 season, when the place was simply called Rust's Lawn. In 1931 it was covered in, and from 1934 to 1939 it was used as a cinema (the 'Olympia'). Concert parties continued to appear there even after World War 2. The building became a roller skating rink in 1948, and was also used for wrestling. It was closed in 1974, and later demolished to make way for Budgen's car park.

Printed ephemera with Pavilion Theatre programmes at the UEA; notes by C. Crawford Holden in Cromer Museum; Peart, The Picture House in East Anglia, p.154.

Pavilion Theatre

One of the earliest surviving programmes for theatrical productions in the Pavilion Theatre is for a 'Pierrotical Fantasy' called the Rolling Stones, in August 1921. After this, 'It was agreed that if possible suitable Theatrical Companies be engaged for about three weeks in August and that earlier and later dates be filled in with Concert Parties.'

Entertainments Committee minutes, 3rd December 1924. The heavy emphasis on 'Concert Parties' continued until the pier was closed in September 1939.

'Cromer Pier Pavilion, which has been closed for 11 years, was reopened last night. When coloured lights, stretching along the pier, were switched on and people began to pass through the gates on their way to the pavilion, pre-war memories were revived.'

Eastern Daily Press, 5th July 1950.

'Crowds turned out in Cromer last night to see the unfamiliar sight of people in Edwardian costume parading through the streets. They also took up vantage points near the entrance to the pier to watch the "Edwardians" going to see the show at the Pier Pavilion.

'The Edwardian dress was brought out to mark the Jubilee of Cromer Pier.'

North Norfolk News, 9th June 1961. The show was 'Summer Song', by the local amateur group.

'The pavilion [is] leased to Mr. T. A. Bolton for £455 a year. . . . There is no heating in the pavilion, acoustics are extremely bad and when a high sea is running the noise is quite intolerable. . . .

'The present lease of the pier to Mr. Bolton runs out next year and "in view of the declining interest from show promoters generally, I think it highly probable that we shall have great difficulty in obtaining an acceptable offer to provide a concert party for 1977 onwards," says the report.'

North Norfolk News, 27th February 1976, p.1, reporting Mr. P. J. Sage's report to the Council's Leisure Services committee. When the committee debated this report, one or two members favoured turning the theatre into a casino but this was fiercely opposed by members who thought it would reduce Cromer to something worse than Yarmouth or Blackpool. The problem of declining audiences was general; Cromer's Regal cinema was due to close at the end of September 1976.

'Most people know I obtained the lease on the pavilion several years ago when the former urban district council decided it was no longer willing to run the summer shows. The strong possibility at that time was that it would be turned into a bingo hall or something similar and then I stepped in and put summer shows on.'

Tom Bolton, speaking at the council's dinner-dance on 19th March 1976 (reported in the North Norfolk News, 26th March 1976, p.2). There was a break in the pattern of summer shows in this year and 1977, when the Alan Clements Theatre Company staged two seasons of plays (with 'Victorian evenings' on Sundays) instead of the usual variety shows. By this time the Town Hall was no longer a theatre.

'North Norfolk District Council have agreed in principle to the spending of at least £25,000 on renovating and redecorating the pavilion . . . all bookings for the theatre will be handled by an organisation headed by Mr. Dick Condon, general manager of the Theatre Royal, Norwich. . . . Mr. Tom Bolton who has leased the council-owned pavilion for the past eight years . . . says that if anybody can make a success of it "it is the Condon organisation." . . . There will be many who seriously doubt whether even the Condon touch can work in Cromer. The district council was faced with . . . a continuing drift leading to collapse or an imaginative and decisive act of faith. . . . It is a bold stroke which deserves to pay off.'

Eastern Daily Press, 14th November 1977. Dick Condon's first season ran from 29th June to 9th September 1978, and he proved so successful that he continued as impresario (working with a succession of young managers) until the 1991 season, when he retired through ill health leaving his assistant Vivian Goff in charge. Nigel Stewart was manager from 1995 to 1997.

Visiting artistes

Some of the better-known artistes who have appeared at the Pavilion Theatre are listed below. A number of them returned on several later occasions.

1910   Fred Chester *comedian*

1921   George Robey *comedian*

1925   Marie Hall *violinist, married to Edward Baring*; Mark Hambourg & Albert Sammons *violinist*

1933   Flotsam & Jetsam

1937   Robb Wilton

1938   Wee Georgie Wood; Vic Oliver

1957   Chris Barber

1960   Semprini; Bryan Johnson

1961   Peter Brough and Archie Andrews *ventriloquist* ; Owen Brannigan *bass*

1964   David Jacobs *compère*

1973   Walter Landauer *piano* ; Bill Pertwee

1978   Humphrey Lyttelton and his band *jazz* ; John Heddle Nash *baritone*

1979   Richard Digance; George Melly; Sandy Powell *79-year old veteran comedian of 'Can you hear me mother?' fame*; Peter Katin *piano* ; Syd Lawrence and his orchestra

1980   Acker Bilk; Frank Ifield; the National Youth Jazz Orchestra; Vilem Tausky and the Palm Court Orchestra; Ian Wallace

1983   Temperance Seven

1987   Max Jaffa

1989   Val Doonican

1995   Midge Ure

1997   Max Bygraves; Danny La Rue; Ray Alan & 'Lord Charles' *ventriloquist*

1998   Paul Daniels *magician;* Fairport Convention *acoustic rock band*

David Jacobs (1964)

Flotsam & Jetsam's autographs collected in 1933 by Beryl Woodhouse

Amateur operatic and dramatic societies

'Although both Cromer and Sheringham each had their individual musical and dramatic societies before the first world war, it was in the year 1923 that members got together and the present Cromer and Sheringham Operatic and Dramatic Society was formed. . . .

'The Society flourished and comic operas, light operas or straight dramas were staged each year, sometimes three in number, right up to the outbreak of the second world war in 1939.' The Society was re-formed in 1949 and staged Gilbert and Sullivan in the Town Hall in 1950 and 1951. The 1952 production - *The Pirates of Penzance* - was the first they put on in the Pier Pavilion - but the very next year this was closed because of the storm damage.

'History of the Society' in 1985 programme.

'First to use the restored pavilion [after the 1953 flood damage] will be a local company, the Cromer and Sheringham Operatic and Dramatic Society, which opens its production of "The Yeomen of the Guard" on Wednesday.'

Eastern Daily Press, 13th June 1955. Thereafter, the Society has maintained an annual production at the Pier Pavilion. The Norfolk Opera Players put on John Gay's The Beggar's Opera at Whitsun 1963, Gilbert and Sullivan's Patience in 1964, and The Gondoliers in 1970.

Children's shows

Johnny Cleveland and Peachey Mead were engaged by Tom Bolton to present a whole summer season of children's entertainment, five afternoons a week, with sponsorship from Rowntree Mackintosh Ltd.

Variety show

'On the large head at the seaward end is an enclosed pavilion, capable of holding a thousand persons, in which are given variety entertainments every weekday evening, and sacred concerts on Sunday evenings.'

Jarrolds' Illustrated Guide to Cromer, 1927. The pattern of a summer variety show during the week, with separate concerts on Sundays, continues seventy years later.

The 'Reds' at Cromer. (Poppyland Collection)

The first 'concert parties' to appear in the new pavilion were the Red Coats and the Middies and Maids, in 1906. At a meeting of the Cromer Protection Commissioners in 1919, `Mr. Willins remarked that during August last year an orchestra was engaged. . . . He personally would rather see an orchestra than variety concerts on the Pier.'

`The Chairman [A. E. Jarvis]: You must take into consideration the fact that at the present time people are not in a frame of mind to sit down quietly and listen to music. They want to be amused. . . . I think it very satisfactory that we have taken just under £100 more last month than we did in the corresponding period last year, when . . . the 25th Division Pierrots were such an attraction.'
Cromer and North Norfolk Post, 5th September 1919, p.5, col.5.

In the 1920s a concert party known as the Rolling Stones played for four weeks in the season. In the 1930s concert parties included the Silver Cameos; Miss Shearson and her Society Entertainers; Fred Hugh and his Paradios; Dennis Redhead and his broadcasting concert party Fools in Fantasy; and Kitt Walter and his Merry Scamps. These mostly appeared for runs of just one week's duration.

The "Out of the Blue" team, in the Sunday Pictorial, 8th August 1937 (Woodhouse Collection)

In 1934 the 'Out of the Blue' concert party, which performed at various towns, began a tradition which in the later 1930s had them putting on as many as seven different shows in the season, changing the programme on Mondays and Thursdays. Their long association with Cromer was interrupted by the war, but continued in the 1950s. A large part of the female population of Cromer seem to have fancied themselves wildly in love with 'Out of the Blue's' tenor, Wilfred Gartrell!

Wilfred Gartrell, one of the heart-throbs of the Pier Show (Woodhouse Collection)

After the flood damage of 1953, the resident summer show was put on in the Parish Hall, only returning to the restored Pavilion Theatre in June 1955, when 'The Bouquets' appeared by arrangement with the London managers Wilby Lunn and Jack Rogers. Their contract was extended for a further two seasons, after which (in 1958) Leslie Sarony starred in a show called 'Over to You!' 'Dazzle', with the Grosvenor Girls, was the summer show in 1959 (reckoned to be the best run for some years) and in 1960 and 1961. Bill Scott-Coomber, a former BBC light entertainments producer, produced 'Tonight at Eight' for the 1962 season, with the Goldway Girls, but it lost over a thousand pounds and fifty people signed a petition calling for the return of 'Out of the Blue'. This show, with a completely new cast of 11 players and two accompanists, returned for an eleventh Cromer season in 1963 and, although it made a small loss, was popular enough to be invited back for the 1964 and 1965 seasons.

'W. C. Fulcher, chairman of the U.D.C., . . . said the Council had been told in no uncertain manner by ratepayers in the town that they wanted "Out of the Blue" back again and, although they did not usually take the advice of the ratepayers, Mr. Fulcher said with a smile, they had not been disappointed. On behalf of the town he thanked the company for their work this summer.

'Producer Dickie Pounds thanked the residents for their support, and said: "It was a very wonderful thought to beg 'Out of the Blue' to return."'

North Norfolk News , 20th September 1963, p.17.

From 1966 to 1969 the summer show was 'Zip A Hoy'. In 1970 Ted Durante and Johnny Cleveland starred in a show with the band-leader Chic Applin; this was followed in 1971 and 1972 by the Ted Durante Show. In 1973 and 1974 the summer show was Robinson Cleaver's 'Showtime', whilst the 'Olde Tyme Music Hall' chaired by George Bolton on two Sunday evenings in 1973 proved popular enough to be put on every Sunday evening in the following season. In 1975 came the Clifford Henry Show. When Dick Condon took over the summer show in 1978 it became 'Seaside Special', directed and choreographed from 1983 by Robert Marlowe.

'"Seaside Special 82" was playing. . . . There were not more than thirty people in the audience that night at the Pavilion Theatre, which was pathetic, because there were nine people in the show. But seeing the show was like observing England's secret life - its anxiety in the dismal jokes, its sadness in the old songs.
'"Hands up, all those who aren't working," one comedian said.'A number of hands went up - eight or ten - but this was a terrible admission, and down they went before I could count them properly.'The comedian was already laughing. "Have some Beechams Pills," he said. "They'll get you 'working' again!"

'There were more jokes, awful ones like this, and then a lady singer came out and in a sweet voice sang "The Russian Nightingale". She encouraged the audience to join in the chorus of the next one, and they offered timid voices, singing,

> Let him go, let him tarry,
> Let him sink, or let him swim.
> He doesn't care for me
> And I don't care for him.

'The comedians returned. They had changed their costumes. They had worn floppy hats the first time; now they wore bowler hats and squirting flowers.
'"We used to put manure on our rhubarb."
'"We used to put custard on ours!"
'No one laughed.
'"Got any matches?"
'"Yes, and they're good British ones."
'"How do you know?"
'"Because they're all strikers!"
'A child in the first row began to cry.
'The dancers came on. They were pretty girls and they danced well. They were billed as "Our Disco Dollies" on the poster. More singers appeared and "A Tribute to Al Jolson" was announced: nine minstrel show numbers, done in black make-up. Entertainers in the United States were arrested for this sort of thing; in Cromer the audience applauded. Al Jolson was a fond memory and his rendition of "Mammy" was a special favourite in musical revues. No one had ever tired of minstrel shows in England, and they persisted on British television well into the 1970s.
'It had been less than a month since the end of the Falklands war, but in the second half of "Seaside Special" there was a comedy routine in which an Argentine general appeared - goofy dago in ill-fitting khaki uniform - "How dare you insult me!"
'I could hear the surf sloshing against the iron struts of the pier.
'"And you come and pour yourself on me," a man was singing. It

was a love song. The audience seemed embarrassed by it. They preferred "California Here I Come" and "When I Grow Too Old to Dream" sung by a man named Derick, from Johannesburg. The programme said that he had "appeared in every night spot in South Africa and Rhodesia". Say "top night spots in Zimbabwe" and it does not sound the same - it brings to mind drums and thick foliage.

'One of the comedians reappeared. I had come to dread this man. I had reason. Now he played "The Warsaw Concerto" and cracked jokes as he played. "It's going to be eighty tomorrow," he said. "Forty in the morning and forty in the afternoon!

"'His jokes were flat, but the music was pleasant and the singers had excellent voices. In fact, most of the performers were talented, and they pretended to be playing to a full house - not the thirty of us who sat so silently in the echoing theatre. The show people conveyed the impression that they were enjoying themselves. But it can't have been much fun looking at all those empty seats. . .

'I stayed until the end of the show, finally admitting that I was enjoying myself. One act was of a kind I found irresistible - the magician whose tricks go wrong, leaving him with broken eggs in his hat and the wrong deck of cards. There was always an elaborate build-up and then a sudden collapse. "Presto," he said, as the trick failed. And then the last trick, the one that looked dangerous, worked like a charm and was completely baffling.

'They saved the saddest song for the end. It was a love song, but in the circumstances it sounded nationalistic. It was sentimental hope, Ivor Novello gush, at the end of the pier that was trembling on the tide. I had heard it elsewhere on the coast. It was anything but new, but it was the most popular number on the seaside that year -

> We'll gather lilacs in the spring agine,
> And walk together down an English lane . . .'

Theroux, The Kingdom by the Sea, pp. 345-348. The show title 'Seaside Special' is said to have originated in a show which Jerry Cottle took around the country in a circus tent some years earlier.

In 1985, a television programme in the *40 Minutes* series was devoted to the Pavilion Theatre. `The millions it reached were impressed. Ever since that programme . . . the Cromer Seaside Special has prospered. . . . As the theatre manager, Andrew Markland, says: "People may or may not come back to Cromer for a holiday. What they will do is come back to see the Seaside Special." . . . Artistes in the Cromer Seaside Special are from the little league; a collection of non-household names. They may not command high fees, but they are a professional troupe - song and dance people in the best tradition. Catch the show if you can. On a hot summer's night in August, the performance is, as usual, sold out.'

Nigel Wigmore, `All together now: there's one end of the pier show that has not ended' in the Guardian, 18th August 1990.

'The fascination of this revival of seaside variety lies in tracking one performer. Take the tall, blond lad. One minute he is pratfalling in a comedy sketch; the next he is an awestruck backing singer in a love song. Now he is dancing in a spangly jacket. And here he is agin, giving us his Ken Dodd before segueing into Max Bygraves, demonstrating all the while the forgotten show-business art of versatility. . . .

'The average age of the audience members is about 60, and their prejudices are precisely targeted. Watching the show, you'd think the war finished only last week, so frequently is it mentioned. Some of the jokes are so corny that you feel the audience must be laughing out of pure gratefulness that they do not contain a swearword. And the show's catchment is limited in another way. "I'd like to think we were getting audiences from all over the country," says [Nigel] Stewart [general manager of the Pavilion Theatre], "but, to be honest, it's the East Midlands."'

Andrew Martin, 'Piers of the Realm' in the Sunday Times colour magazine, 25th August 1996, p.3.

Summer Shows on the pier

Only those in bold type were on for more than one week

1921	Rolling Stones
1922	**Rolling Stones**; Tweenies; Versatiles
1932	West End Revellers
1933	Curios; Pier Revellers
1934	**Out of the Blue**
1935	**Out of the Blue**
1936	**Out of the Blue**
1937	**Out of the Blue**; Seamews; Society Entertainers; Town Topics; Merry Scamps; Clacton Revelry; there was also a summer Fayre from 15th to 22nd May
1938	**Out of the Blue**; Merry Scamps; Society Entertainers; Fools in Fantasy
1939	**Out of the Blue**; Red Rays; Fools in Fantasy; Merry Scamps Paradios; Society Entertainers
1940-50	Pier closed by the war
1951	**Out of the Blue**; Gaities
1952	**Out of the Blue**; Stardust
1953-54	Pier closed by the floods
1955	**The Bouquets**
1956	**The Bouquets**
1957	**The Bouquets**
1958	**Over to You**
1959	**Dazzle**
1960	**Dazzle**
1961	**Dazzle**
1962	**Tonight at Eight**
1963	**Out of the Blue**
1964	**Out of the Blue**
1965	**Out of the Blue**
1966	**Zip A Hoy**
1967	**Zip A Hoy**
1968	**Zip A Hoy**
1969	**Zip A Hoy**
1970	**Chic Applin Show**
1971	**New Ted Durante Show**
1972	**New Ted Durant Show**
1973	**Showtime**
1974	**Showtime**
1975	**Clifford Henry Show**
1976	Season of plays instead of summer show
1977	Season of plays instead of summer show
1978-	**Seaside Special**

SOURCES

Where no source is mentioned, information is generally derived from the minutes and accounts of the Cromer Protection Commissioners or from programmes, newspaper reports or advertisements.

Books and articles

Adamson, Simon. *Seaside piers*. London: Batsford, 1977.

Bacon, Nathaniel. *The official papers of Sir Nathaniel Bacon of Stiffkey, Norfolk, as Justice of the Peace, 1580-1620*. London: Royal Historical Society, 1915. (Camden Third Series, vol. 26).

Bacon, Nathaniel. *The papers of Sir Nathaniel Bacon of Stiffkey*, edited by A. Hassell Smith and Gillian M. Baker. Norwich: NorfolkRecord Society, 1983, 1990.

Banville, Larry. *The Banville diaries: journals of a Norfolk game keeper 1822-44*. Edited by Norma Virgoe and Susan Yaxley. London: Collins, 1986.

Bayne, A.D. *Royal illustrated history of Eastern England*. Yarmouth: Macdonald, [1888?]. (Written over a period of several decades.)

Blanchard, E. L. *Adams's descriptive guide to the watering places of England, and companion to the coast*. London: W. J. Adams, [1848; another edition, 1851].

Brooks, Peter. *Coastal towns at war: the story of Cromer and Sheringham in the Second World War*. Poppyland Publishing, 1988.

Buxton, Elizabeth Ellen. *Ellen Buxton's journal 1860-1864*. London: Geoffrey Bles, 1967.

Calendar of State Papers Domestic.

Cromer and Sheringham. 1921. (Burrows Guides)

Cromer - sketched. 1859. (Galley proof in the Norfolk Record Office, COL/13/171.)

Cromer Urban District Council Act 1948 (11 & 12 Geo. 6). (Copy in Norfolk Record Office in MS 21604, 479 x 8.)

Dent, H. C. *The reminiscences of a Cromer doctor*. Holt: Norfolk Press Syndicate, 1923? (Reprinted from the *Cromer and North Norfolk Post*.)

Durst, David W. 'Hase: Ironfounder of Saxthorpe,' *Journal of the Norfolk Industrial Archaeology Society* vol. 6, no. 1 (December 1996), pp. 69-87.

Eastern counties collectanea, I (1873), pp. 37-39.

Excursions in the County of Norfolk. London: Longman, 1818. 2 vols.

Goodwyn, E. A. *Cromer past*. N.d.

Harper, Charles G. *The Newmarket, Bury, Thetford, and Cromer Road: sport and history on an East Anglian turnpike*. London: Chapman & Hall, 1904.

Hewitt, W. *An essay on the encroachments of the German Ocean along the Norfolk coast with a design to arrest its further depredations, dedicated to the Right Honourable the Lords Commissioners of the Admiralty*. Norwich: Matchett, Stevenson & Matchett, 1844.

History and antiquities of the county of Norfolk. Norwich, 1781.

Holden, C. Crawford. *A history of Cromer lifeboats*. 1975. (Unpublished typescript in Cromer library)

Holiday notes in East Anglia, being a selection of articles which have appeared in the public press on the holiday resorts in Norfolk, Suffolk, and Essex. Stratford: Great Eastern Co., 1886.

Holiday notes in East Anglia, being a selection of articles which have appeared in the public press on the holiday resorts in Norfolk, Suffolk, and Essex. Stratford: Great Eastern Co. 1894. [Same title, but this edition is a completely different selection of articles]

Hooton, Jonathan. *The Glaven ports: a maritime history of Blakeney, Cley and Wiveton in North Norfolk*. Blakeney: Blakeney History Group, 1996.

Illustrated guide to Cromer. Jarrolds, 1927. [Revised edition of Knights.]

Ketton-Cremer, R.W. *Forty Norfolk Essays*. Norwich Jarrold, 1961.

Ketton-Cremer, R.W. *Country neighbourhood*. London: Faber & Faber, 1951.

Knights, Mark. *The Illustrated guide to Cromer and neighbourhood . . . revised to the present time*. New edition, London: Jarrold, [1890]. [Revised version of Alice Sargant's *Guide* of 1841.]

Lewis, Samuel. *A topographical dictionary of England . . .* 7th ed. London: Lewis, 1849.

Lockwood, Nancy. '"The best of all the sea-bathing places": the story of Cromer pier.' In *Norfolk Fair*, November 1975 pp. 24-25; December 1975, pp. 18-19; January 1976, pp. 10-11.

Mackie, Charles. *Norfolk annals: a chronological record of remarkable events in the nineteenth century (compiled from the files of the 'Norfolk Chronicle')*. Norwich: Norfolk Chronicle, 1901.

Oppenheim, E. Phillips. *Those other days*. London: Ward Lock, 1912.

Parliamentary debates (Hansard).

Peart, Stephen. *The picture house in East Anglia*. Lavenham: Terence Dalton, 1980.

A pictorial and descriptive guide to Cromer . . . 8th ed. London: Ward Lock, [c.1925].

Pigot and Co.'s national commercial directory . . . Norfolk & Suffolk. London & Manchester: J. Pigot & Co., 1830.

Rouse, Michael. *Coastal resorts of East Anglia: the early days*. Lavenham: Terence Dalton, 1982.

Rye, Walter. *Cromer, past and present*. Norwich: Jarrold, 1889. (This is the most detailed account of the earlier history of the various piers at Cromer, though the papers of Nathaniel Bacon were not available to Rye.)

Rye, Walter. 'Notes on the Port and Trade of Cromer alias Shipden.' *Norfolk Archaeology*, 7 (1872), pp.276-288. Contains the original form of the text from the Patent Roll which mentions Cromer pier.

Sargant, Alice. *A guide to Cromer and its neighbourhood, by a visitor*. Cromer: Leak, 1841. (Published anonymously, but an inscription in the copy once owned by the Hansell family and now in the possession of R. C. Fiske shows that it was written by a 'Miss

GEORGE ROBEY

George Robey, who signed this card when appearing at Cromer (Woodhouse Collection)

Sergeant' of Hackney, who kept a finishing school for young ladies.)

Sargant, Alice. *A guide to Cromer and its neighbourhood, by a visitor.* 2nd ed, 1851.

Sargant, Alice. *A guide to Cromer and its neighbourhood, by a visitor.* 5th ed, 1867

Savin, Alfred Collison. *Cromer in the County of Norfolk: a modern history.* Holt: Rounce & Wortley, 1937.

Scott, Clement. *Blossom land and fallen leaves.* 2nd ed. London: Hutchinson, 1890.

A short history of Tissington and its parish church. Tissington, n.d.

Theroux, Paul. *The kingdom by the sea.* London: Hamish Hamilton, 1983; Penguin, 1984.

Universal British directory of trade, commerce, and manufacture. . . London, [1791]. Vol. 2.

Walcott, Mackenzie E. C. *The East coast of England from the Thames to the Tweed.* London: Stanford, 1861.

Warren, Martin. *Cromer: the chronicle of a watering place.* North Walsham: Poppyland Publishing, 1988.

Windham, William. *Diary 1784 to 1810.* Edited by Mrs Henry Baring. London: Longmans, Green, 1866.

Newspapers

Cromer and North Walsham Post, continued as *Cromer & North Norfolk Post*

Cromer, Sheringham and District Weekly Press

Eastern Daily Press

Guardian

Lloyds List

Norfolk Chronicle

Norfolk Daily Standard

Norfolk News

North Norfolk News

Norwich Argus

Norwich Mercury

The Times

The Sunday Times

Yarmouth Gazette

Archives, manuscript sources and ephemera

Patent Roll 14 Ric II (2nd part), membrane 44 (Public Record Office: C66/332)

Account of money received by George England from John Blowfield for building material and labour for the pier at Cromer, late 16th/early 17th century (Norfolk Record Office: MS 20403, 126 X 6)

Playbill of 1822 (Cromer Museum)

Anonymous diary of the 1820s (Norfolk Record Office: MS 80)

Mr Marten's diary (Norfolk Record Office: MC26/1, 504 X)

Minutes of meetings concerning application in 1845 for an Act of Parliament (Norfolk Record Office: BIR 213)

Letter from John Wright to the Committee for the Protection of the Town of Cromer, 28th February 1845 (with plan L4526 at the Hydrographic Office, Taunton)

Letters and papers of Simeon Simons relating to the Goldsmiths' School in Cromer (in the collection of The Worshipful Company of Goldsmiths)

Cromer Protection Commissioners' minutes and accounts, and Entertainments Committee and Works Committee minutes (Norfolk Record Office; Cromer Museum; Cromer Town Council offices)

Letter of 13th June 1910 from W. T. Douglass to the Cromer Protection Commissioners, with related notes and newspaper cuttings (Norfolk Record Office: DC 1/4/50)

Valuation Office fieldbook (Public Record Office IR58/62396, hereditament no. 355)

RNLI Précis Book

Edw. Boardman & Son, architects, of Norwich. Plans for proposed restaurant etc., 1948 (Norfolk Record Office: drawings 157/B and 157/D in BR 35/2/56/1). Also files of correspondence and accounts relating to the reinstatement of the pavilion etc. after the 1953 flood damage (BR 35/3/4194)

North Norfolk District Council. Report of the Chief Executive and Clerk to the Cromer Pier Working Party, 6th May 1992.

C. Crawford Holden's notes on Cromer history. (Cromer Museum)

Martin Warren, unpublished notes on the history of Cromer pier. 1990. (Cromer Museum)

Miss D. B. Woodhouse's notes from personal memories and from the minutes of the Cromer Protection Commissioners (now in Cromer Museum)

Maps and pictures

Prints, photographs and drawings in Cromer Museum Crawford Holden Collection

Sketchbooks belonging to R. C. Fiske of Morningthorpe Hall: two dated 1820-2 and another dated 1863 with sketches of Cromer and neighbourhood.

Cromer protection: plan of proposed jetty, sea-wall and other defences, 1845 (Hydrographic Office: L4526)

Cromer promenade pier: plans and section. Session 1867. Engineers:Jerram & Boswell. (Norfolk Record Office: C/Scf1/609)

Cromer pier: plan and section. Session 1884. Engineers: J. F. Puttick, F. H. Cheesewright, Westminster (Norfolk Record Office: C/Scf1/614)

Cromer esplanade pier: plan & section. Session 1887-8. Engineers: G. B. Nichols & Son, London E.C.; Geo. B. Jerram, London E.C. (Norfolk Record Office: C/Scf1/619)

Cromer sea protection - proposed foreshore improvements. Plan to accompany report by Messrs. Coode, Son, & Matthews, dated 28th May, 1892. (Photocopy in Cromer Museum)

Engineers' plans of 1899 (Cromer Museum)

No. 58. Bandstand, drawing no. 10/536, scale 1:24, by David Rowell & Co. Ltd. (Norfolk Record Office: DC 1/1/21)

Plans and elevations of the 1900 pier shelters and entrance gates, the 1904 design for roofing in the enclosure, the 1948 proposals for a restaurant and 1949 extension to the pavilion. Architects: Edw. Boardman & Son. (Norfolk Record Office: BR 35/2/56/1-4).

Cromer & Sheringham Operatic & Dramatic Society's production of 'The Yeomen of the Guard' on the pier, 1955.

INDEX